W9-AHH-086

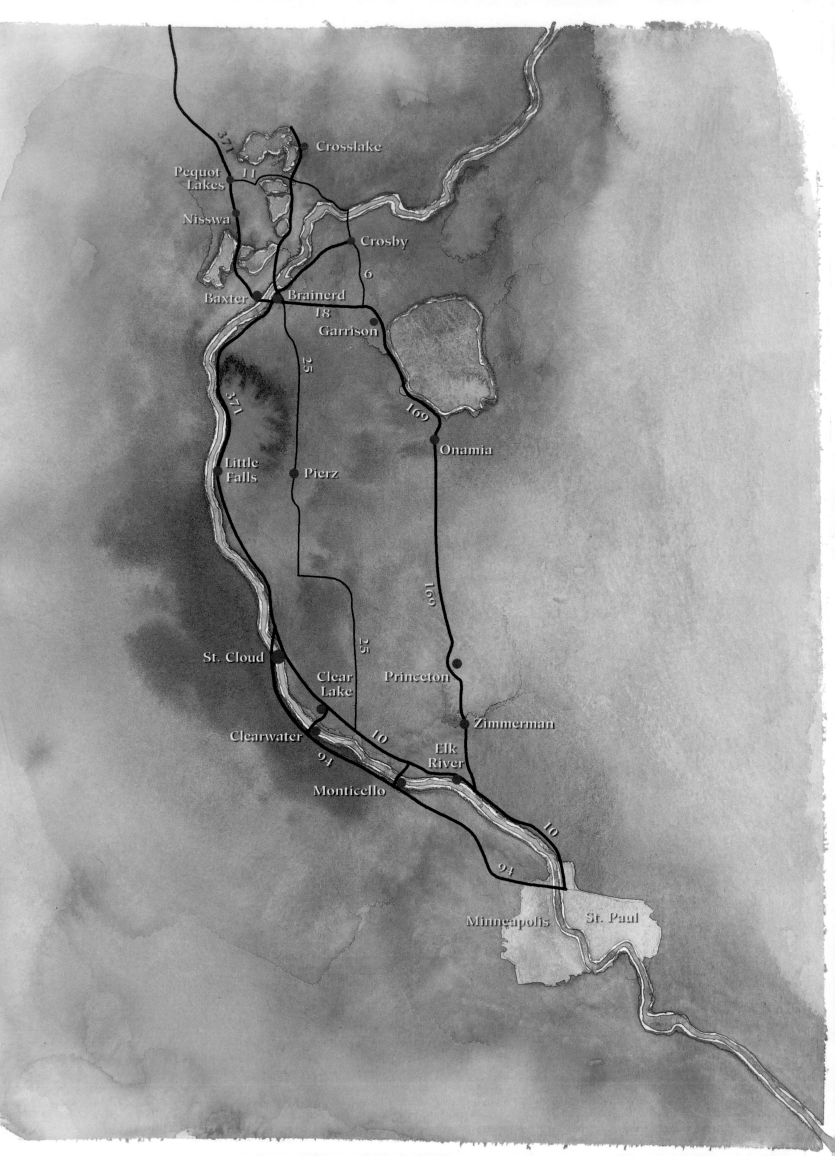

BRAINERDBOUND

landmarks to the lakes

Mark Rustad   Curtis Johnson   Mark Utter

Published 2004	Landmark Publishing Inc Box 46403 Minneapolis, MN 55446
Copyright 2004	Landmark Publishing Inc
ISBN	0-9726738-0-6
SAN	254-9689
Library of Congress	2002095934
Senior Photographer	Curtis Johnson Curtis Johnson & Associates
Graphics and Design	Nelson-Mitchell Advertising Outfitters 7393 Clearwater Road Baxter, MN 56425
Printer	Bang Printing 3323 Oak Street Brainerd, MN 56401
Website	Midwest Captions 150 Birchridge Drive Brainerd, MN 56401
Project Director	Mark Rustad
Managing Editor	Mark Utter

All rights reserved.   No part of this work may be reproduced or used in any form by any means without written permission from the publisher.

www.BrainerdBound.com

Thousands of years ago the glaciers receded and left a multitude of lakes and rivers in Central Minnesota. Pine forests soon flourished. This combination of ubiquitous waterways and pine forests was a major factor in the subsequent exploration, development, and habitation of the area. For over a thousand years, men and women have traveled to Central Minnesota by foot, horse, wagon, boat, train, car, and plane.

BrainerdBound: landmarks to the lakes is dedicated to these generations of travelers past, present, and future who share a common thread: an overwhelming passion for this lakes area.

It was the authors' repeated trips to their cabins and the intriguing landmarks they saw through their car windows that gave birth to the concept of creating this picture book. Initially the concept was to provide a portrait of the countless landmarks that dot the major highways to the Brainerd Lakes area. In the rush to get to our Brainerd area destinations, we rarely take the time to stop and explore the landmarks on our repeated trips to the northwoods.

The scope of the book was later expanded to include the key events, people, and history of this vacationland. We hope this expanded perspective enables you to better discover a certain connectedness between the people, places, and eras covered in this book. You will discover how today's tourism is connected to the people and events of the past.

We quickly learned what a daunting task it was to compile an all-inclusive photo journal about the history, tourism and the drive north into the Brainerd Lakes region of Central Minnesota. After capturing 30,000 images for this book's consideration, our editing room floor was covered with enough pictures and storylines to fill yet another book.

Our goal is to balance our coverage and to please as many of our readers as possible. Ultimately, we hope to increase your appreciation for the drive up north and to bring a smile to your face as you travel to the Brainerd Lakes area one page at a time.

Billy Utter plays an early morning round at The Pines

Twenty thousand holes are drilled twenty-four hours before the 13th annual Brainerd Jaycees Ice Fishing Extravaganza

Hailed as two of the world's best all-around anglers, brothers Al (pictured) and Ron Lindner moved their families from big-city life in Chicago to Brainerd in 1967. The Brainerd Lakes area was chosen over others because of its abundance of lakes and rivers within a two-hour drive and the variety of fish species available. Together they pursued their dream of careers in the sport fishing world. Their list of accomplishments include co-founding Lindy Tackle and In-Fisherman, winning over fifty awards in tournament fishing, and producing innovative fishing programming, including Lindner's Angling Edge, seen nationwide on local broadcast and cable channels.

Ron and Al have been shining the spotlight on the Brainerd Lakes area for over 30 years, helping transform the area into one of the most popular fishing destinations in Minnesota. Both have been inducted in the National Freshwater Fishing Hall of Fame as well as the Minnesota Fishing Hall of Fame. One of the duos most treasured accomplishments has been their involvement of family in their many businesses, spawning the next generation of accomplished Lindner's. Al and Ron's sons have graced the covers of major fishing publications and have become accomplished photographers, producers, and tournament fishermen.

Nisswa's annual CITY OF LIGHTS and fireworks celebration

PAUL BUNYAN
STATE TRAIL

Studded
Tracks
Allowed
Next
1 Mile

Fishing launch on Lake Mille Lacs

Before there was Brainerd, there was Crow Wing; a town that at its peak boasted a population of nearly 700. Built along the confluence of the Crow Wing and Mississippi Rivers, it was the site of battles that would establish Ojibwe control over the Dakota tribe for hunting and fishing rights. French fur traders reached the area by the 1770s. Trade relations were established with the Indians as permanent trading posts were built along the rivers' banks.

The settlement became a popular replenishing point for the traders moving goods back and forth from St. Paul to Winnipeg along the famed 600-mile Red River Oxcart Trail. One of Crow Wing's chief residents was a mixed blood French Ojibwe fur trader named Clement Beaulieu. His landmark home is seen here. Today, the town is gone but the home is showcased inside Crow Wing State Park. Built in 1849, it is the oldest standing structure found anywhere in Minnesota north of the Twin Cities.

By the 1850s, Crow Wing transitioned from fur trading to logging. The town's riverbank landscape was marked with hotels, saloons, warehouses, trading posts and blacksmith shops. In 1858, Minnesota became the nation's 32nd state, drawing two of its eighteen original representatives from this town of Crow Wing. Nine years later, the Ojibwe residents of Crow Wing were relocated to the White Earth Indian Reservation.

While the fur trading and logging industries combined to build this historic village, the railroad industry caused its demise. Northern Pacific Railroad selected a site nine miles to the north to cross its tracks westward over the Mississippi River. As residents moved upstream for new jobs and a new beginning, the town of Crow Wing was abandoned.

John Gregory Smith, then Governor of Vermont, was named President of the Northern Pacific Railroad. Starting near Duluth, the new railroad laid track to the west, reaching the banks of the Mississippi River in 1871. It was there that a new rail town was established, named after Smith's wife Anna Eliza Brainerd.

On July 2, 1864, Abraham Lincoln signed an Act of Congress creating the Northern Pacific Railroad Company. The railroad was chartered to connect the Great Lakes to Puget Sound following the trails mapped by the Lewis and Clark expedition. Twenty thousand men worked from 1870-1883 to complete the project.

Vital to the completion of the railroad were the Northern Pacific rail shops built and left behind in Brainerd. They serviced the locomotives, rail cars and more than 2,000 miles of track for Northern Pacific. By 1880, Crow Wing was gone, while more than 1,000 men worked for the Northern Pacific shops in Brainerd. By 1920, more than eighty percent of Brainerd's population was still employed by the railroad industry, with resort tourism beaming on the horizon.

Stewart C. Mills, Sr. providing guided tours on Gull Lake.

The birth of tourism in the Brainerd Lakes area dates back to the late 1800s when new railroads first brought migrating loggers, miners and recreational anglers through the region. Visitors sought local farmers for direction, food and lodging.

The earliest and most popular destination was the home of Joseph and Josephine Ruttger on Bay Lake. When Josephine's legendary cooking began to draw crowds, the Ruttger family decided to start charging for food and lodging. As a result, Ruttger's Bay Lake Lodge was established in 1898. This was the first resort in the Brainerd area and remains today the oldest family-run resort in the state of Minnesota.

With Brainerd's rail shops flourishing and the pine forests leveled, logging moved north as the family-run resort industry began to grow. Stewart C. Mills, Sr. delivered logs from Nisswa to Gull Lake, where he helped build the lake's first resorts, including Anderson and Rocky Point. He later guided tourists on Gull Lake and delivered the mail.

Following World War I, Stewart C. Mills, Sr. purchased the Lively Auto Company in Brainerd and went into the car business. He formed the Mills Motor dealership in 1931. He and his wife Helen K. Mills and their sons Stewart C. Mills, Jr. and Henry C. Mills II opened a farm supply store called Fleet Wholesale Supply in 1955. Five years later, they changed the name to Mills Fleet Farm.

Grand View Lodge was built in 1919, around the time Helen K. Mills graduated from Carleton College. One of her classmates was Brownie Cote, who later purchased Grand View Lodge and founded Camp Hubert for girls and Camp Lincoln for boys on nearby Lake Hubert. The resort's history can be felt by visiting the original main lodge which is listed today on the "National Register of Historic Places."

By 1922, Billy Fawcett, a Twin Cities based publisher of the famed comic book *Captain Billy's Whiz Bang*, began construction on a resort on Pelican Lake called Breezy Point. Billy was an eccentric millionaire who built the resort as his fly-in playground for the rich and famous. After the main lodge burned down in 1959 and was rebuilt, Brownie Cote purchased the resort, which was later sold to a group headed by Bob Spizzo in 1981.

The post-Depression era of the 1930s saw tourism in Minnesota explode. The state ranked third in the nation behind Florida and California as a travel destination. With automobile touring on the rise, recreational development sites and family run resorts were building momentum. There were now more than 1,200 lakeside resorts in Minnesota vying for business. Several new resorts, lodges and hotels were surfacing throughout the Brainerd Lakes area, especially around the Whitefish Chain and the south side of Gull Lake.

Alex Ruttger, son to Joseph Ruttger, built the Brainerd Lakes area's first golf course adjacent to the family resort on Bay Lake in 1921. In 1926, two Kansas City businessmen built Gull Lake's first golf course, adjacent to the Roberts Pine Beach Hotel. By 1932, this course was leased to Tom Madden and his nephew Jack Madden. They also purchased Mission Point Resort, which is now Madden Lodge. Jack and his younger brother Jim Madden then became partners and purchased the Roberts Pine Beach Hotel, building the resort to its present size of 300 rooms. Madden's on Gull Lake is in its third generation of operation by the Madden family.

The Maddens brothers were considered pioneers in the Brainerd resort community. They influenced many fellow family-run resorters, including Sherman and Mae Kavanaugh, who started Kavanaugh's Resort and Restaurant in 1969.

Merrill K. Cragun, Sr., a good friend of Jack Madden's, saw the benefit of drawing more tourism to central Minnesota. Merrill promoted the first annual Brainerd Paul Bunyan festival and registered ownership of the name "Paul Bunyan Inc". With the help of his wife Louise and his father Virgil Cragun, Merrill built a few cabins on the south end of Gull Lake. Cragun's Resort officially opened for business the day after Pearl Harbor was attacked. By 1947, the resort had grown to twelve cabins and a main lodge. Ten years later, son Merrill Cragun, Jr., better known as "Dutch", became

manager. With his wife Irma by his side, the two have operated Cragun's Resort and Hotel on Gull Lake ever since.

By 1950, the Baby Boom generation began to flood even more families into the resorts of Minnesota's north woods. Post war tourism spiked the state's tourism revenue to more than $200 million. Brainerd strengthened its association with Paul Bunyan when Sherm Levis and Roy Kuehmichel opened the Paul Bunyan Center to entertain vacationers. Larry and Eliner Lopp operated the gift store there and later purchased the park from Sherm Levis. Working on opening day was daughter Patti Lopp. She later married Don McFarland and together they purchased the Paul Bunyan Amusement Center from her parents and operated it until it closed in 2003.

Along with countless others, these legendary Brainerd Lakes Area families combined to build the base of tourism that the region enjoys today. To honor their names, we captured the portrait on the following page at the historic Lake Hubert Train Station. It was here, a century ago, where vacation seekers disembarked from Northern Pacific trains to enjoy an "up north" adventure. We honor and thank these families.

Pictured standing from left to right are Jack Ruttger, Stewart C. Mills, Jr., Dutch Cragun, Don McFarland, and John Kavanaugh. Sitting are Deb (Madden) Thuringer, Bob Spizzo, and Mary (Cote) Boos. Many of the parents and grandparents of this group of area luminaries founded resorts, tourist attractions, and businesses that lured travelers to the Brainerd Lakes area.

BRAINERDBOUND

landmarks to the lakes

Whitefish 30-51

U.S. Highway 10 52-87

Landmark Tributes 88-97

Cuyuna Range 98-117

U.S. Highway 169 118-127

Mille Lacs 128-141

State Highway 371 142-181

Gull Lake 182-219

neighboring WHITEFISH

Bob Hanson: Minnesota Office of Tourism's Fishing Ambassador

While most Brainerd area vacationers take part in sports associated with the summer, such as golfing, boating and fishing, some prefer to take to the ice. The Brainerd Lakes area is host to numerous prestigious hockey and figure skating camps, including the ones held at the Breezy Point Ice Arena. The Minnesota Wild hosted a training camp for twenty-two eager hockey players battling to make a spot on the preseason lineup. Pictured on the right is 6' 7", 250-pound Derek "Boogyman" Boogaard, once hopeful Minnesota Wild player, now intimidating forward for the Wild's primary developmental minor league affiliate, the Houston Aeros. Brawn is replaced by beauty when Caitlin Staab, a graceful figure skater enrolled in the *Point of Perfection Figure Skating Camp*, takes the ice.

Since 1978, the Ideal Fire Department Beef and Corn Feed has been held on the 2nd Wednesday in August. The event brings the community together and raises funds for the Ideal Fire Department Relief Association. Proceeds help equip the twenty-two volunteer firefighters who protect Whitefish area residents and cabin owners. Over 2,000 people from the lakes region eat over 10,000 cobs of corn, and 1,800 pounds of beef. The father of Chief Ron Schultz donates the corn, homegrown on his nearby farm.

The tradition of Bean Hole Days was initiated in 1938 when a group of businessmen wanted to thank the local farmers for their harvest with a fall festival. Held the Wednesday after the 4th of July in Pequot Lakes Bobberland Park, the tradition has continued annually with the exception of a brief interruption during World War II. Five mammoth cast iron pots of beans are lifted from the ground around 11:45 a.m. after being baked in the ground since the "Lowering of the Beans" ceremony the night before. Thousands gather to taste the delicious beans, congregate with new and old friends, listen to music, and shop at the Arts and Crafts Fair. Kimberly Larson, Miss Pequot Lakes/Crosslake 2003, is active in Pequot Lakes' area festivities.

In the late 1960s the already flourishing fishing industry turned competitive and the modern fishing tournament format was spawned. Gull, Whitefish, Cross, Pelican, Mille Lacs and other area lakes began hosting major walleye, northern pike, and bass tournaments during the four seasons. Pictured here is the 2003 Gander Mountain Invitational Bass Tournament held on the Whitefish Chain.

Professional fishermen participating in area tournaments include nationally recognized anglers Al and Ron Lindner, Babe Winkelman, Gary Roach and Marv Koep. Many other professional tournament anglers also make their home and compete in the Brainerd Lakes area, including Bob Hanson, Ted Takasaki, Perry Good, Tom Whitehead and Rich Boggs.

Brainerd was established as a result of the railroad industry pushing west and served as a center for the logging industry pushing north. By 1900, timber had become Minnesota's biggest industry. The state was blanketed with pine trees, some white pines reaching heights of 200 feet. The Gull Lake and Northern Railway built tracks into the woods north of Brainerd to help harvest and extract logs, while the Mississippi River fed the timber to the sawmills downstream. The lumber was used to lay the bed for the nation's rail tracks, and helped build homes, schools and churches across America.

More than 20,000 lumberjacks worked the logging camps at the timber industry's peak, producing 2.3 billion board feet of lumber each year. Their working conditions were miserable. By 1905, the Department of Health ordered all camps to be burned to the ground to prevent the spread of smallpox. By 1918, Brainerd's forests had been leveled and logging operations moved north.

Joey Erickson
Rush Lake

Jim Spielman of Pequot Lakes attached a chainsaw motor and homemade gear box to a power ice auger. On January 11, 2003, Jim drilled three holes through 18" thick ice in 11.5 seconds on Pelican Lake, and was crowned the first ever World Power Ice Auger Champion at Breezy Point's annual Ice Fest.

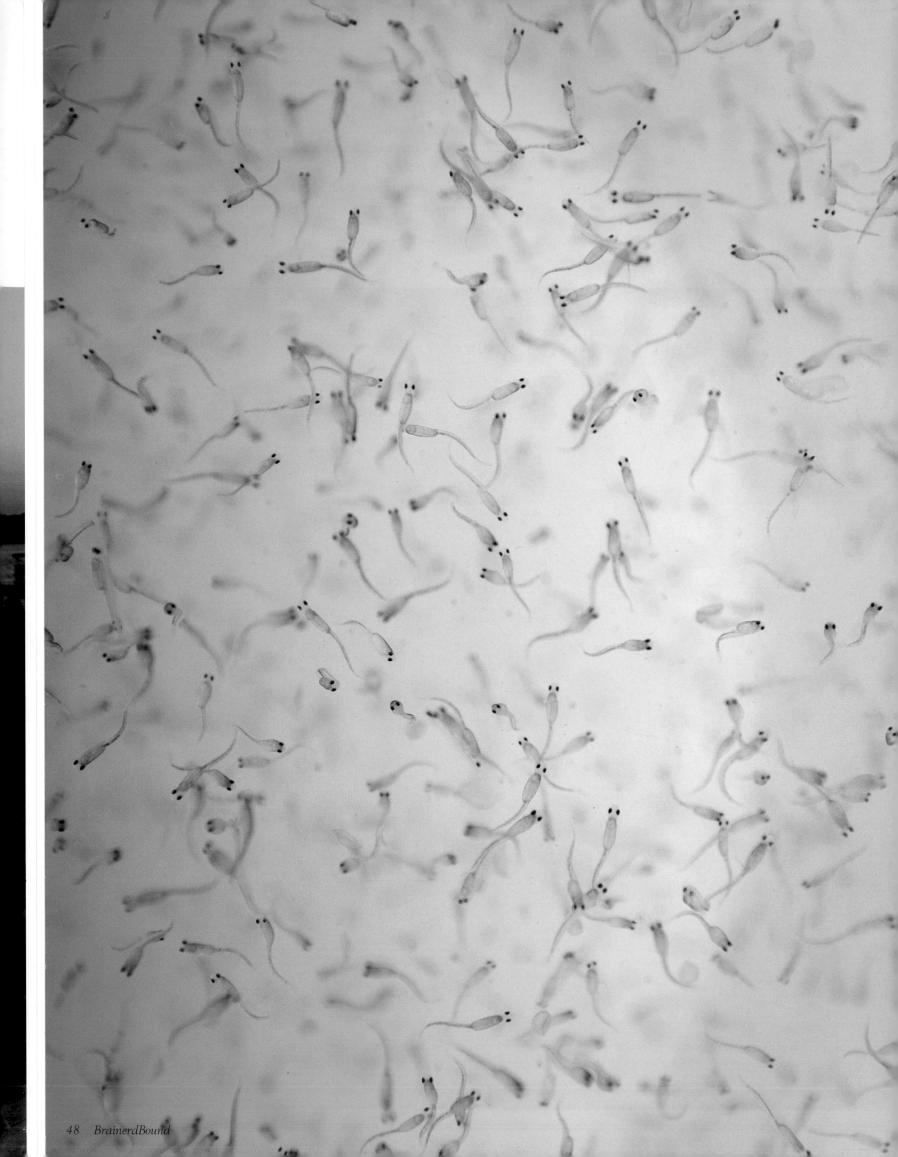

The Minnesota Department of Natural Resources (DNR) has been assisting local anglers by stocking walleye fry in the Brainerd area lakes since the 1920s. In the spring, approximately 85 million eggs are stripped from female walleyes in the Pine River and brought to the DNR Hatchery in Brainerd for placement into incubation containers. In roughly three weeks the eggs hatch into fry and await their turn to be deposited into the area lakes. Although less than 1% of the fry typically survive, there will be hundreds of thousands of additional walleye lurking around area lakes due to the stocking program. DNR Fisheries Specialist Mike Knapp releases 627,000 walleye fry into Round Lake.

In 1991, the U.S. Dept of Transportation established the National Scenic Byways program designed to unite matching government funds with local grass roots community efforts for enhancing and promoting highway routes of exceptional interest. Four years later, a raffle was held in Ideal Township to raise funds for the improvement of bicycling conditions along County State Aid Highway 16. The roadway was then nominated to receive National Scenic Byway designation in hopes of securing matching federal funds. As a result, today's Paul Bunyan Scenic Byway is recognized as one of only twenty such byways in the state. The 54-mile picturesque drive weaves through the Whitefish area, linking historic resorts, bikeways, hiking trails, wildlife areas, wetlands and breathtaking views.

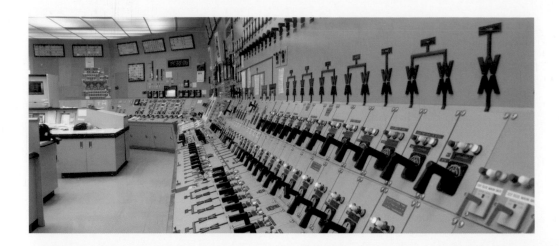

One of the most visible landmarks you see on the horizon when driving to the lakes country is the Sherco Generating Plant's twin stacks towering 650 feet into the sky in Becker, MN. Built in 1975, this is the largest coal burning plant in the Xcel Energy fleet. Three times each day a dedicated Burlington Northern Sante Fe train delivers an average of 120 carloads of coal. Each car contains more than 100 tons. Eleven miles of conveyer transport the coal, which is crushed into powder and blown into large boilers burning at 2,500 degrees. The fuel converts two million gallons of water per hour into steam, which in turn powers large turbines that create enough electricity to power 2.4 million homes.

While the trains return empty to the mines of Wyoming or Montana, where a 300-year supply awaits their refill, the steam from the Sherco stacks billows harmlessly into the skies over Becker.

Doug Huseby was first introduced to the furniture business in the 1970s. He soon became convinced that he could supplement his income as a stock broker by selling furniture. On his first attempt, he sold seven truckloads of furniture in seven hours, enough to convince him to switch careers. To control overhead, Doug moved his first furniture warehouse from Minneapolis to Becker, and the rest is history.

Becker Furniture World opened its doors in 1978 in a modest 500 square foot facility. Today that store has expanded to over 300,000 square feet, making it the largest furniture showroom in the state. Along with Doug's wife Julie, and their boys Jim and Joel, the Huseby's attribute their success to their 300 employees who share their common vision. Their store is meant to serve as a destination; a place where kids can play, families can eat, and parents can shop a variety of price ranges. While their customer base extends nationwide, their proximity to U.S. Highway 10 heading north to Brainerd makes for a favorite destination among Minnesota's cabin owners.

More than 79,000 farms landscape Minnesota's rural highways. Combined, they produce more than $7.5 billion in agricultural cash receipts, ranking Minnesota sixth in the nation in crops and livestock. Art Peterson owns one of those farms. In 1955, he bought 160 acres of land in Big Lake and began growing potatoes.

Over the past half century, Art has watched his business expand to cover more than 2,000 acres of land bordering the west side of U.S. Highway 10 south of Becker. From July through October Art harvests more than 23 million pounds of potatoes.

Protecting Minnesota's crops against disease, insects, weeds and nutrient deficiency rests in the hands of crop-dusting pilots like Craig Oleen. His familiar yellow spray plane can be seen all summer long dancing in the skies from Big Lake to Little Falls. He flies his plane five feet above the ground spraying more than 3,000 acres a day for customers like Art Peterson.

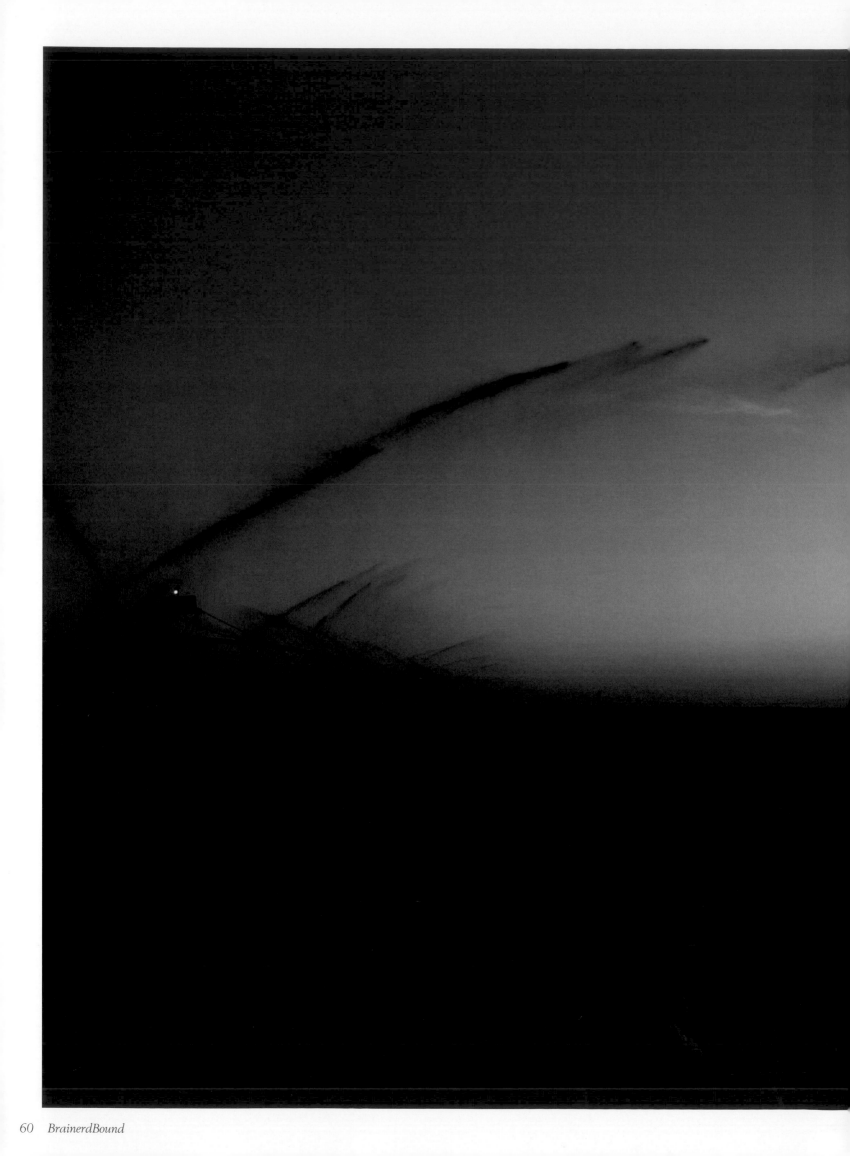

Buried deep beneath today's superhighways to the north are water veins left over from the glacial ice age. Landmark irrigation systems that decorate those beautiful sunset drives to the lake country are seen tapping into these veins and spreading up to 1,000 gallons of water an hour over Minnesota's agricultural landscape.

Founded by Don and Rose Nelson in 1976, the
Clearwater Travel Plaza is located at Interstate 94
and Minnesota Highway 24, which is the busiest
intersection in Minnesota during the summer
weekends. The Food Network featured Clearwater
Travel Plaza in *The Best of...* series as one of the top
five truck stops in the country. Each year as many as
1 million travelers stop by to fill their vehicles with
gas or diesel, or fill themselves with a homemade
meal, a fresh bakery product, a loaf of world famous
Nelson Bros. Fritter Bread - or purchase a unique
Minnesota gift.

Tom Boelz has been a resident of Clear Lake since 1960, living in a house built in 1898. This seems very appropriate for the area's leading Clear Lake historian. Tom can tell you all about the oxcarts that used to travel near Clear Lake bringing merchandise to the riverboats for transport to St. Paul or how the city by the lake moved to its current location in 1868 when the St. Paul Manitoba rail line was built. Stop by Tom's Amish Furniture Shop where he has been selling furniture for 30 years and while you're browsing through the Amish furniture, you may get a Clear Lake history lesson.

◄ John Leo "Angus" McDonald opened McDonald's Meats in 1914. As a general store for the Clear Lake area they sold groceries, meats, and delivered ice for refrigeration. John Leo's son Dick stood at the helm from 1952 until 1989 when his son Dave took over and changed the name to *McDonald's Meats - The Jerky Stop*. With grocery store chains now expanding into their markets, Dave worried about the store's future. He was the third generation to run the family store and wanted to pass it on to his son, Travis. Hiring a consultant to provide advice on how to keep the store viable, he discovered the winning ticket: jerky. Dave added a smokehouse and started making 5 pounds a day. Dave's kids gave out free jerky samples to the passing cars in front of their store on Highway 24. McDonald's now smokes 1,000 pounds of beef, turkey, and pork weekly. Many a Brainerd-bound traveler stops at McDonald's to step back in time and pick out a choice piece of meat for the lakeside barbeque, to buy a unique package of jerky, or just to chat with the friendly butcher.

An anonymous elderly couple stood staring at the waterfalls as Rodger Johnston turned to greet them. They informed Rodger that their only son had been killed in Viet Nam, and that his body was never returned to them. Their monthly visit to the *Falls of Our Fallen* memorial in St. Cloud was their way of keeping his memory alive.

Rodger explained to the elderly couple that the memorial was built in dedication to the veterans, law enforcement officers and firefighters who died while protecting and serving our country and our communities. He pointed to the bronze eagles perched above the falls, positioned to take flight and deliver the soul of one of the fallen to their final resting place.

What Rodger didn't tell the couple was that he is CEO next door at the American Heritage National Bank, which sponsored the memorial he personally designed and built.

The Minnesota Office of Tourism currently operates or partners with eleven Travel Information Centers in the state of Minnesota. They are designed to assist long-distance travelers, and help promote local tourism.

The St. Cloud facility seen here was built atop a farmstead that dated back to the early 1900s. When the Center was built in the 1990s, the farm was lost, but the silo was preserved to honor the area's agricultural heritage.

Allison Johnson joins well-wishing friends Kayla and Casey Jedele at the Clemens and Munsinger Gardens in St. Cloud. Tucked along the eastern banks of the Mississippi River, the Munsinger Garden is a fourteen-acre informal garden paradise that dates back nearly a century. For contrast, the Clemens Gardens were built in the 1990s. This formal set of six gardens rest high atop a sunny hill across the street to the east, proudly displaying perfectly manicured garden beds that surround some of the state's most beautiful outdoor water fountains. These gardens are a collective feast for the senses, and well worth a visit on your next trip to the lakes.

The St. Cloud Correctional Facility is the second oldest and fifth largest of the eight state prisons in Minnesota. The first seventy-five inmates were received from Stillwater in 1889. The original purpose of the St. Cloud facility was to serve as a reformatory for first-time offenders, ages 16-30. The distinction was made between punishment and reform in an attempt to help redirect the lives of younger males through job training and character development.

The prison structure was developed in stages between the years 1887 and 1926. Cellblocks, administrative offices, training buildings and the massive prison wall were all built by the inmates using the granite stone cut from two quarries on the prison grounds. The construction of these buildings was considered among the finest in the country at the time due to their excellent sanitary conditions and resistance to fire.

More than a century later, these same buildings remain relatively unchanged.

Today, the St. Cloud prison houses more than 800 inmates and serves as the intake facility for the seven all-male prisons in Minnesota. Any convicted felon sentenced to serve time in the state will first be sent to St. Cloud. Upon evaluation, the inmate will be re-assigned to the facility that best fits his needs and his sentence. Each month, an average of 300 inmates are relocated to another facility.

St. Cloud is a level four security prison, equal in rank to Stillwater. The only level five security prison in Minnesota is Oak Park Heights. The average inmate at St. Cloud is 31 years old, serving a 42-month sentence at a taxpayer cost of $80 per day.

Patt Adair has served as the Warden at the St. Cloud Correctional Facility since 1995. Her career began as a social worker in the Twin Cities. While working with troubled youth, she developed and taught a series of parenting classes for the adults, designed to reinforce her work with the kids. When the Shakopee Women's Correctional Facility got word of Patt's classes, they hired her to teach the same to the mothers in prison. After working there for ten years, Patt was promoted to the rank of Assistant Warden.

Today Patt walks fearlessly down the spotless corridors of the St. Cloud Correctional Facility as the prison's first female warden. She directs a staff of 400 who help manage a prison population count of more than 800 level four offenders. While Patt demands mutual respect between inmate and guard, her leadership has delivered results. Today, four of the state's eight prisons are run by women.

Nominated by her staff, Patt was voted Minnesota's Department of Corrections Employee of the Year in 2001. While her husband supports her career, their grandchildren are still too young to know what grandma does all day.

Positioned eighty feet above the floor of the prison yard, this panoramic view from Guard Tower 9 unlocks the mystery behind the great granite wall of the St. Cloud prison. The wall stands twenty-two feet tall, measures four feet thick at its base, and surrounds fifty-five acres of land that once served as the prison's own granite quarry. It is the second largest continuous wall built by penal labor found anywhere in the world. The largest is the Great Wall of China.

"The Mystery of Minnesota's Wall"

"Daddy, what is that big gray wall for?" These words resonated through my nine year old mind time and time again, as my family traveled up Highway 10 on numerous excursions from Bertha to the Twin Cities. Yet somehow the words were never voiced. It wasn't a silly question for a child to ask his father, but perhaps it was something more; the wonder, the awe, the immensity of this massive conglomeration of concrete & mortar, the mystery of what could possibly lie beyond such an incredible structure. At 60 miles per hour, a boy's mind tends to wander into realms of wonder, and this wall created such opportunity for my imagination.

Today I again see that wall. Though years have passed, the aura still remains. However, today the mystery takes on a completely different form. It is one that few would scarcely wish to experience, nor to view with their own eyes. Perhaps my vision can enlighten the mystery behind this great wall.

Beyond the big gray wall is a park. At first glance a seemingly ordinary park. There lies a lawn with fresh cut grass, the greenest of Minnesota's green. Dozens of geese float lazily upon the soft ripples of a deep blue pond, the deepest of Minnesota's blue. There are baseball fields, basketball courts, a newly paved walking track, and tables scattered throughout this park behind the wall.

Beyond the park is a hill. Not too steep, yet a hill nonetheless. I've climbed it many times, though oft hesitantly I confess. Beyond the hill lies a building with a locked door, an enormous building of concrete gray. A tower looms overhead, and one cannot help but feel the eyes from above watching him. Beyond the locked door lies a hallway. A brilliantly lit hallway with a shining floor and a vast endless corridor. Walking down the hallway, cameras hang from above. Though some may ignore this realization, one feels the intensity of unknown spectators observing his every step.

Beyond the hallway are brown metal doors. Not an ordinary door as in a home or office, but a heavy solid door that slams with even the slightest effort. Beyond the solid door lies a world, a plethora of humanity, a "community" if you will. One hundred sixty rooms, though "room" seems too pleasant a word. Each cell is surrounded with three concrete walls and a front made of solid bars, each bar painted cream-white to mask its iron.

Beyond the iron bars stands a man. Perhaps he was once America's most wanted. Perhaps he is now America's least wanted. He is a man of robust stature. He stands quietly, 240 pounds of muscle and flesh, built by his daily regimen in the weight room. He rarely speaks, which makes his countenance one that is seen but not heard. By some he is respected, by others he is deeply feared.

Beyond the iron bars a man sleeps. He lays upon a three inch mattress atop an iron slab, six feet long and thirty inches wide. Upon this bunk the man dreams, a melange of fishing poles and flashing lights, a mother's voice and wailing sirens. He can awaken at the slightest uncommon sound, yet slumber through the changing keys and the slamming of doors.

Beyond the iron bars a man reads a novel. The cover is missing and perhaps a few pages from within, but he doesn't mind the tattered condition. For he is reading words, not a story. His mind cannot absorb the images written by Hemingway, Twain or Grisham, for his thoughts are a million miles from the story before his eyes.

Beyond the iron bars a man yells. Not the hurtling yell of a frightened lamb, but that of a frightened child trapped in a grown up body. He yells to the man across the way, to the man below him, to anyone he thinks will hear his voice. The man knows that the shrillness from his lungs will bother the others, yet he pretends not to care. After all, does he believe anyone could possibly care about him?

Beyond the iron bars a man writes, and though he doesn't expect an answer to his words, he will send the letter anyway. Another man endures the pain of a dragon-shaped tattoo, while the newest resident stares in awe at this monotonous task. One man carries his bible wherever he goes, perhaps in faith, perhaps in fear that he will become a target if he were to leave it behind. Another man's eyes dart to and fro, his edginess is no longer provoked, it has become instinctive.

Beyond the iron bars a man's head is buried beneath a dark blue pillow, for no one can see his tears there. Behind the iron bars are souls of much diversity. Some are not really living, they are merely existing. There are men who hope, men who despair, men who are thoughtless, men who care. Some who watch television twelve hours a day, some who make license plates to pass the hours away. Some go to high school, Vo-tech, college too, men who hold visions where life will one day become new. They embrace the same hope, they share a similar dream, they find their own way to do time, not allowing time to do them.

Today I stare at that big gray wall, and the aura still remains. I think of the tens of thousands who have lived behind the wall, and the tens of thousands who travel past it each day. Behind this wall, men from all walks of life have come and gone. I often wonder if another man may have stood on this very same spot and pondered my very same thought. Perhaps it was one of the "younger" brothers from the notorious Jesse James Gang imprisoned here. Or maybe a simple father, a grandfather, or a mother's only son.

As a boy, I often dreamed and wondered what could possibly lie beyond the big gray wall. As a man behind that wall, I again wonder. I dream of what is on the other side, of a changed world much different than I can recollect. I wonder if that old barn on the way to town ever fell over, or if the spruce I planted as a child has survived 25 harsh Minnesota winters. I wonder if people still make their own maple syrup, if grandmother still makes lefse, or if she would even recognize me. I wonder what it feels like to walk alone in the woods, to hear a squirrel chatter, to see a fawn in spring.

The next time you drive past that big gray wall and wonder what is on the other side, consider that a man is likely wondering what is on your side. This is a phenomenon that has existed for more than a hundred years, and might very well continue for a hundred more. The big gray wall isn't merely a structure, it is a part of Minnesota, a part of history, and a part of every life that has seen the wall from either side.

The adult education class inside the St. Cloud Correctional Facility agreed to participate in an essay contest for this book. The inmates were asked to write a letter describing life behind bars. The winning entry seen here remains anonymous upon request.

E.M. Helgeson founded the St. Cloud Hatchery in 1926. In the beginning, its main business was selling day-old chicks to farmers throughout the Midwest. By the 1950s, the company had transitioned into broiler chicken production. By 1983, it became a fully integrated poultry company, overseeing all aspects of production and marketing of its chicken products.

Today, Gold'n Plump is the largest producer of premium chicken products in the upper Midwest. It operates three processing plants, two hatcheries and two feed mills at locations in Minnesota and Wisconsin. The company employs more than 1,500 people and contracts with nearly 300 independent growers. CEO Mike Helgeson, the grandson of the founder, is continuing the company's history of innovation and market leadership. The Gold'n Plump feed mill and elevator in Sauk Rapids stand on opposite sides of U.S. Highway 10 en route to Brainerd. Up to 1 million chicks each week are hatched at Gold'n Plump's St. Cloud facility.

David Watts likes to describe the beginnings of his Little Rock Boat Works as a "Cinderella story." He started following his passion for refurbishing antique boats in the early 1980s when he was still working for St. Cloud Prison. He began working on wooden boats in his garage after work. In 1986 he opened Little Rock Boat Works and dedicated himself to creating these wooden masterpieces full-time. His accomplishments include winning the Thunderbird Award at the world famous Lake Tahoe National Boat Show and the People's Choice Award at the annual Whitefish Chain Antique and Classic Wood Boat Show. David and his skilled craftsmen restored this 1960 thirty-two foot Chris Craft owned by Bob White.

Anyone who has traveled on Highway 10 through Royalton will recognize Treasure City. It has been a favorite stop for children and adults alike since 1962. Robert Janski revels in his daily interactions with these loyal customers who enjoy browsing through the endless array of treasures. Many longtime customers will recount to Robert their childhood memories of the larger-than-life 300-pound clam, the *surprise packages*, or any of the numerous favorite items they remember from their childhood and are then heartened to see are still there.

BABE THE BLUE OX

PAUL BUNYAN CENTE

BRAINERD MINNE

For fifty-three years the twenty-seven foot tall lumberjack Paul Bunyan stood bigger than life, an enduring icon of the Brainerd Lakes area. Paul has enchanted generations of children by chatting with them and calling them by name. The fifteen-ton Babe the Blue Ox wasn't always at his side, arriving fifteen years after Paul. Pictured here is Nate Whited, a frequent voice of Paul during the 1970s and 1980s, during the last thirty minutes Paul Bunyan Amusement Center was open. Another notable voice of Paul is Dave Borash, a current Brainerd High School History and Geography teacher. Dave wrote his Master's thesis on the Paul Bunyan Amusement Center's impact on the cultural landscape of the Brainerd Lakes area, and was the voice of Paul for seventeen years.

HELICOPTER
VIEW THE BRAINERD LAK

NO
SMOKING

HELICOPTER
TICKETS
SPECIAL $14.95
EACH!

BIG ELI
10

Mini Himalaya

dippin dots   Ice Cream
Store

WA FAMILY FUN CENTER 13MI.

DON'T MISS

Paul's Sweet Tooth

Olde Tyme Photo

BATTING CAGES

BUNK HOUSE

COOK SHACK

PAUL BUNYAN EXPRESS

OPEN 10am - 7pm Daily
OUR LAST YEAR!

PAUL BUNYAN

Paul Bunyan Amusement Center
1950 - 2003

On Monday, September 1, 2003, Paul Bunyan Center closed for good, breaking the hearts of Minnesota residents and the many vacationers who had visited the park in past years. The summer of 2003 gave parents one last chance to bring their children to Paul Bunyan Amusement Center and gave local communities and organizations, including the Governor of Minnesota, a chance to fight for Paul and Babe's survival. A summer of uncertainty turned to hope when This Old Farm, only eight miles east of Brainerd, was finally chosen to be Paul and Babe's new home. On Friday, September 19, Paul and Babe left their home of fifty-three years and made their historic journey to This Old Farm.

Four generations of Rademachers have toiled to assemble this fifty-acre tribute to yesteryear. It is one of the few remaining public attractions that capture the area's history of farming and pioneer living. Paul Bunyan Land at This Old Farm Pioneer Village showcases antique cars, a blacksmith shop, a print shop, old farm machinery and implements, a fire station, general store, filling station, grainery, log house, one room school house, saw mill, saloon, depot and many other classic structures that will bring you back to the Brainerd of the early 1900s. To add to the heritage, Paul Bunyan, Babe the Blue Ox, and over thirty rides and attractions will be added beginning in 2004. Two-year-old Ethan Ringold of Maple Grove finds great joy with the more traditional aspects of This Old Farm.

BRAINERD BOUND
Landmarks Lost

Deer Forest/Bambi Land

Gull Drive-In Theater

Paul Bunyan Amusement Center

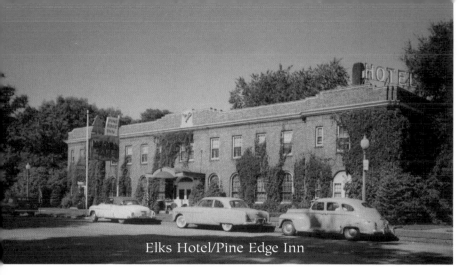

Elks Hotel/Pine Edge Inn

Ak-Sar-Ben Gardens

"KNOWN FOR GOOD FOOD"
AIR-CONDITIONED
BRAINERD, MINNESOTA

Van's Café

Lumbertown U.S.A.

Fort Mille Lacs

neighboring

CUYUNA RANGE

Cuyler Adams lived from 1852-1932. As an employee of the Northern Pacific Railroad, he brokered a stock purchase in the company for a group of investors, and used his commission to buy land near the new railroad tracks in Deerwood. While his intent was to harvest timber and supply railroad ties back to Northern Pacific, his plans would soon change. While mapping the woods to determine property lines, strange deflections in his compass signaled iron ore underground. Drilling began in 1903.

Today, the Croft Mine in Crosby stands as a living memorial to Cuyler Adams and the mining industry that built the Cuyuna Range. Open to the public, the park features the red house seen here, which was Cuyler's original office. The neighboring mine shaft provides a simulated underground history lesson for everyone. The name Cuyuna was derived from "Cuy" of Cuyler Adams and "Una," his dog that accompanied him on his early land explorations.

Of the three iron ore ranges in Minnesota that combined to produce eighty percent of the world's iron ore, only two could produce the raw material in magnetized form. This was the preferred pelletized version of ore that converts more profitably to steel. When Cuyuna's ore was found to be non-magnetized, the last underground mine ceased operations in 1968.

Left in the wake of these abandoned strip mines were huge 500-foot deep craters surrounded by banks of earth standing 200 feet tall. Today these hills have become forested with aspen, birch, pine and maple trees, while underground water veins have transformed the former mining pits into some of the cleanest fresh water trout fishing lakes in the Upper Midwest.

Today more than twenty-five miles of undeveloped lakeshore property line the pit lakes. The Cuyuna Country State Recreation Area was formed to protect this 5,000-acre parcel of land from developers. Controlling canoeing, fishing, camping, hiking and horseback riding are all efforts designed to provide public access to the lakes while preserving their natural settings. Today, plans are being developed to link the area by bike path to the Paul Bunyan Trail. The new path weaving around the pit lakes will be called the Cuyuna Lakes Trail.

Bill Matthies has owned and operated Minnesota's School of Diving in Brainerd since 1959. Shortly after he opened the school, he was asked to assist in recovering a Buick from the bottom of Portsmouth Lake in Crosby. His exposure to the water's clarity on that dive opened a door to scuba enthusiasts throughout the Upper Midwest.

Today more than 250 scuba divers dive every weekend during the summer in the clear waters of the Cuyuna Range pit lakes. Bill uses the variety of dive sites to train and certify both recreational and commercial divers. He also hosts weekly dive excursions, and caps off each season with an annual underwater pumpkin carving contest.

In 1958, a 34-year-old Major in the U.S. Air
Force named Dr. David G. Simons climbed
aboard a small sealed capsule at the bottom
of the Portsmouth Mine in Crosby,
Minnesota. The gondola was tied to the
bottom of a polyethylene balloon filled with
three million cubic feet of helium. The
project, labeled Manhigh I, was one of a
series of manned balloon launches
conducted to measure human reaction to
space travel.

Dr. Simons became the first man to ever
reach a height of 100,000 feet, landing
thirty-two hours later in a farm field in North
Dakota. He became the first human in
history to see the sun set and then rise again
from the edge of space.

Two farmers stopped into the Cuyuna Bar in the summer of 1978. Each discovered the other had a tick on him. The bartender suggested they race them across the top of the bar. One year later, the second annual tick race was declared with invitations sent to a motorcycle club in St. Cloud. The bar changed its name to the Woodtick Inn, and today plays host one Saturday each June to more than 450 bikers, 1,000 spectators and 150 ticks. The owner walks the ditches for weeks preceding the event and saves all the ticks that collect on her legs.

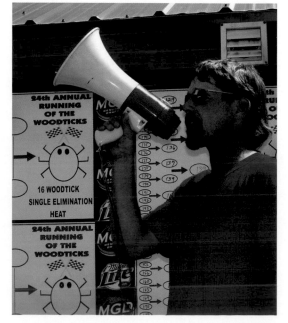

Ruttger's Bay Lake Lodge hosted its first annual Oktoberfest celebration in 1986. Owner Jack Ruttger sought to celebrate the season's harvest while honoring his family's German heritage. His grandfather Joseph, original founder of the resort, was born in Neulinengen, Germany where the Ruttger winery was started in 1643.

Today, more than 7,000 people return each year to enjoy the festival, shop among 150 vendors, and be entertained by the likes of the Bavarian Dancers and the Concord Singers. What once was a simple celebration has turned into Ruttger's biggest grossing weekend of the year.

Forty years ago the American Bald Eagle count in the contiguous United States dropped to fewer than 400 nesting pairs. As a result of pesticides and lead poisons being passed along through the food chain, the eagle's eggshells became too thin for routine incubation and were crushed by the nesting mother. By 1973, the raptor would be included in America's first ever list of endangered species.

Today these raptors symbolize not only America's freedom, but also the best of what our wildlife conservation efforts have to offer. For many years, Minnesota's Department of Natural Resources transported baby eagle chicks from nests in northern Minnesota and relocated them to other states to help restore our country's eagle population counts. Thanks to efforts like these and heightened public awareness, the American Bald Eagle has rebounded sharply. Today, there are more than 7,000 nesting pairs in the country, with more than 700 in Minnesota. At the time of this printing, forty nesting pairs reside in Crow Wing County.

Feeding off the clean waters in the Brainerd lakes area, this beautiful bird reaches a top speed of over 50 miles per hour. The male weighs an average of eight pounds, while the female averages twelve pounds. Their white heads and yellow beaks do not show color until they reach five years of age. They stand up to three feet tall and carry a wing span of up to seven feet. With an average life span of more than twenty years, American Bald Eagles mate for life and return to the same nesting area each year. Their nests can weigh as much as one ton.

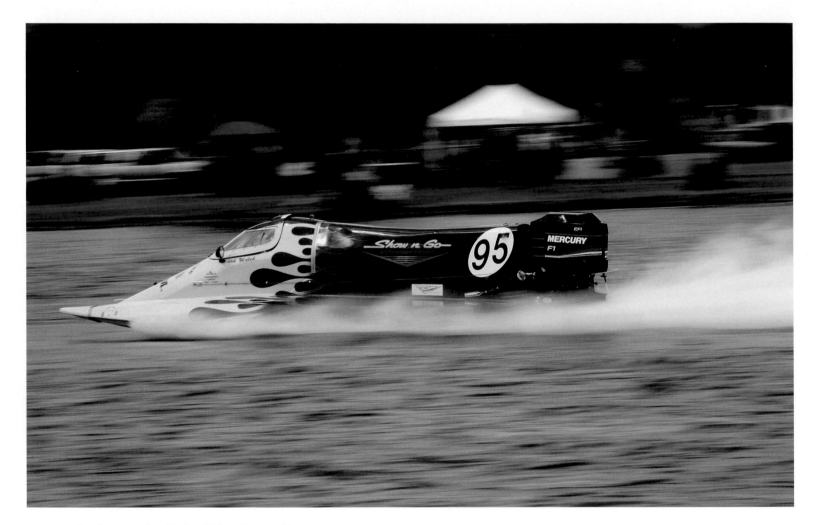

Each year the Twin Cities Power Boat Association hosts a weekend of high powered speed boat racing on Serpent Lake in Crosby. High performance racing boats with stock 25 horsepower to modified 350 horsepower engines, measuring twelve to seventeen feet in length, race at speeds in excess of 100 mph. Shown here is the SST120 boat owned by Mark Welch of Wayzata, MN. Mark was the US-1 High Points National Champion in the Mod-U class in 2003.

In 1862, Abraham Lincoln signed into law the Homestead Act. This declared that any citizen could claim a 160-acre plot of government surveyed land as their own, so long as they agreed to build a home on the land and cultivate crops. After five years, they received title to the land free of charge.

One such homesteader was Henry Knieff of Bay Lake Township. As the Northern Pacific Railroad pushed west establishing the towns of Aitkin, Deerwood and Brainerd, odd-numbered plots of land along both sides of the railroad were offered as inducements to investors. The even-numbered sections were awarded to local homesteaders. Henry selected the site along the north shore of Bay Lake, where grandson Albert still lives today. Seen here in his homemade boat, Albert surveys the shoreline awarded to his grandpa more than 120 years ago.

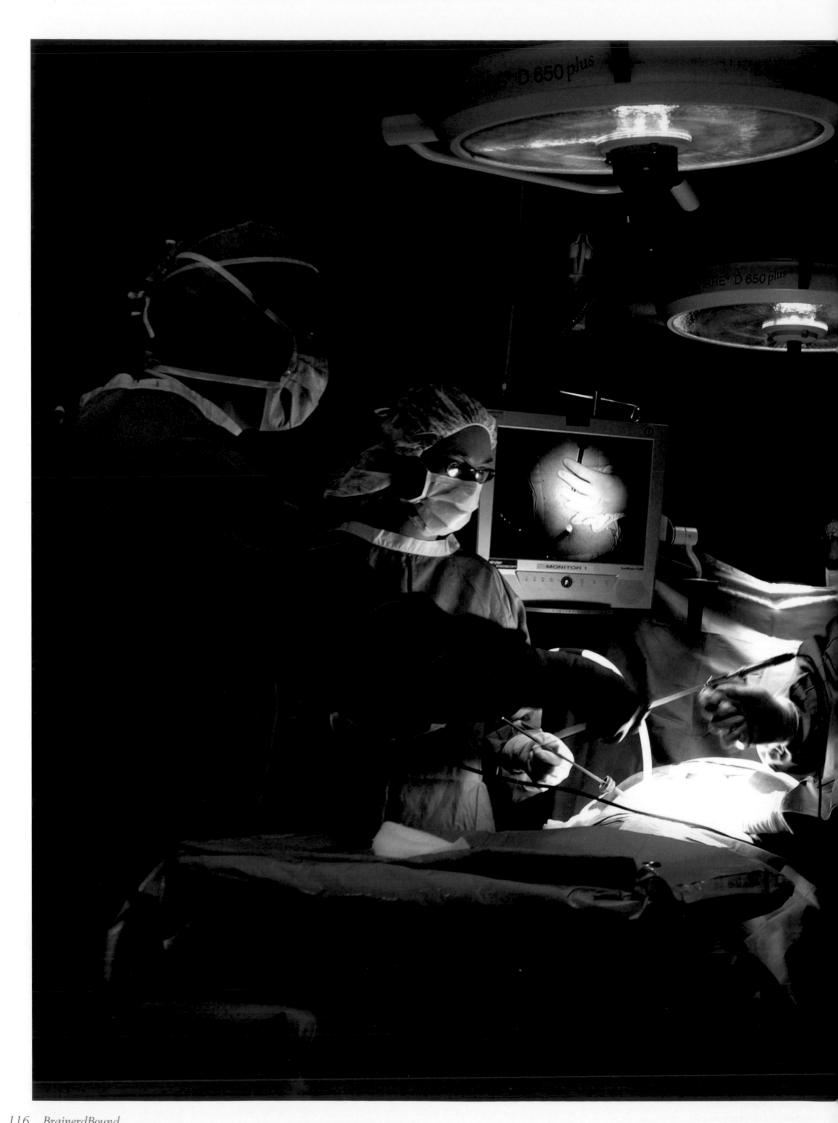

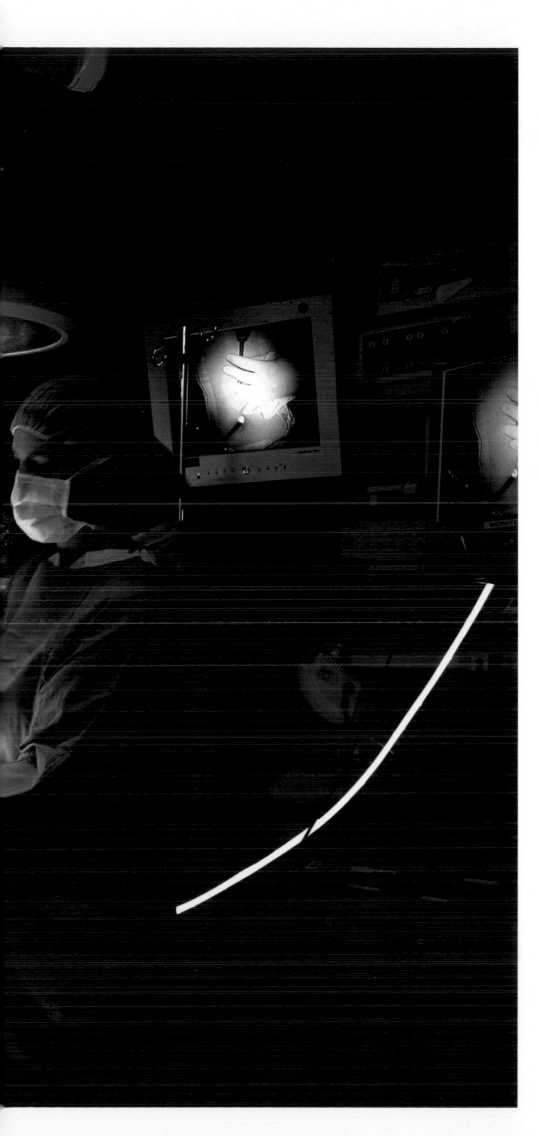

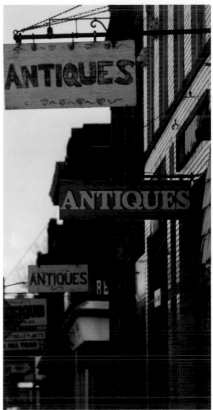

The old storefront and antique shops of Crosby speak to a time when the small towns and mines of the Cuyuna Iron Range boomed and immigrant miners and their families flocked to the region for good jobs, fair wages and a better life.

The mines have played out. The old pits are lakes now. And while Crosby today is known as the Antique Capital of Minnesota, it is also home to the Cuyuna Regional Medical Center. This is an ultra high-tech medical campus that provides sophisticated state-of-the-art primary care even as surgeons perform dazzling minimally invasive procedures and advise and consult surgeons elsewhere, even in third-world countries, such as Haiti, in real-time via telemedicine.

The southern-most landmark covered in *BrainerdBound* is the Oliver Kelley farm. This 189-acre living farm pays tribute to yesteryear, as the farming practices of Oliver Kelley and family date back to the 1870s. Interpreters dress the part and help educate today's youth as to the farming practices of more than 100 years ago.

Specialty bred plants and animals of the era fill their gardens, fields and barnyards, including non-hybrid seeds for planting and old style Berkshire hogs.

Standing four feet tall, the Greater Sandhill Crane is one of the biggest and most beautiful birds in North America. They spend their summers as far north as Hudson Bay, and winter along the Texas Gulf and in Central Florida. Each year, thirty-five pair nest in Sherburne National Wildlife Refuge where more than 2,000 of these birds will rest and feed during fall migration. Their presence is a direct result of a team of dedicated biologists who work to restore this 30,600-acre refuge to the natural habitats of a century ago in order to draw wildlife back to the area. Sherburne is one of over 540 refuges in the National Wildlife Refuge System, committed to the conservation of wildlife, under the direction of the U.S. Fish and Wildlife Service. The refuge has walking and driving trails open to the public. All are reminded to respect the animals and their habitat, take only memories and leave only footprints.

Native Prairie
Seeded 1993

While there are more than 500 retail nursery and garden stores in the state of Minnesota, few are as large in scope as Princeton-based Nelson Nursery. Set along U.S. Highway 169 en route to Brainerd, owner Mike Lemke supplies more than twenty of his statewide retail outlets with flowers grown here under cover of more than four acres of greenhouses.

Owner Todd Benedict opened Northbound
Antiques in 1994. One board at a time, he
lifted the siding off a barn built in the 1880s
to create this unique storefront nestled along
U.S. Highway 169 in Milaca. Today more
than twenty dealers compete for floor space
in this popular antique store so appropriately
named. Three of every four customers that
stop in are north bound travelers seeking
authentic items for their cabins.

A favorite personality along the *BrainerdBound*
drive is Lloyd Jacobson of Creative Wood
Products. For more than twenty years, set along
U.S. Highway 169 in Milaca, this former cabinet
maker turned farmer has used the highway to
market his woodworking projects to his
cabin-bound audience. While his signature
pieces are his handmade wooden windmills,
Lloyd confesses that he pulls more traffic off the
road with his hay bale sense of humor seen here!

Each Monday from April through July, up to 50,000 pheasant chicks are hatched at the Oakwood Game Farm and shipped overnight to customers throughout the country. Jim and Betty Meyer have been raising these birds in captivity since 1967 at their 100-acre ranch, which is among the largest bird propagation facilities in the United States.

As a result of Franklin D. Roosevelt's National Recovery Act of the 1930s, thousands of young men were put to work around the country building steel fire towers for detecting and combating forest fires. Over a thirty-year period, more than 150 were built in northern Minnesota. Today, less than forty remain standing, including this 100' tower located inside the Mille Lacs Kathio State Park.

Seen here from the tower is the shoreline of Lake Mille Lacs. It serves as the source to the Rum River, which snakes its way through the park en route to the Mississippi River more than 140 miles downstream. Kathio is the fourth largest of Minnesota's sixty-six state parks, covering more than 10,000 acres of land which offer the visitor trails for horseback riding, hiking, and cross-country skiing.

Housing more than 1,500 video slot machines with more expansion coming, the Grand Casino Mille Lacs averages daily slot payouts in excess of $1 million. Combined with its 350-seat bingo hall, 29 blackjack tables, and year-round entertainment booked into their grand concert schedule, the gaming facility draws more than two million visitors every year.

There are 3,600 members of the Mille Lacs Band of Ojibwe. One-third of them live in the vicinity of Onamia where the casino is located. While each member receives revenue from the casino, the amounts are modest. The bulk of the casino revenue is invested in the future of the Mille Lacs Band of Ojibwe and their non-Ojibwe neighbors through the development of schools, clinics, housing and retirement centers, government centers and a tribal police department.

Garrison Sports is one of more than forty launch fishing services on Lake Mille Lacs. Charter boats, locally called launches, dock at resorts around Mille Lacs and offer a unique big-water and big-boat fishing atmosphere for charter groups and walk-on passengers. Launch captains supply all the needed fishing equipment to catch everything from perch and walleye, to muskie, northern pike, and smallmouth bass.

Launch fishing grew up in the 1930s as guides and resorters discovered good walleye action on the previously unexploited offshore mud flats and deep gravel bars. While the captain does his best to ensure the kids catch fish, the launches are a welcome relief for those parents who would otherwise spend their boat time untangling lines and baiting hooks!

Imported from Germany, windsurfing was first introduced into the United States in 1978. Within five years, Lake Mille Lacs began hosting an annual windsurfing race called the Crossing. Seen here is Vojta Cervenka of Hanover, MN. Reaching top speeds of up to 50 mph, Vojta fights the winds with a sixteen-foot mast and five-meter sail. He is a world-class windsurfer, having twice been invited to compete for a spot on the U.S. Olympic Windsurfing Team.

As the waters of Lake Mille Lacs freeze over, the local Garrison Sports Club welcomes the annual return of the World Snowmobile Association Extreme Ice Races. For more than twenty-five years, Mille Lacs has hosted the event, a favorite stop among the top 100 world-class ice racers who compete on the circuit. Seen here is Harvey Otremba of Wyoming, Minnesota, completing his qualifying run on this half-mile oval track by reaching top speeds of more than 100 miles per hour.

Migration marks the change of seasons on Mille Lacs. As trailers pack up and head south for the winter, Ring-billed Gulls gather at the end of the Garrison Sports dock to prepare for flight. Their winters are spent scavenging along the east coast of the United States, from New England to the Gulf of Mexico.

Minnesota ranks first in the nation per capita with more than two million anglers registering for their annual fishing licenses. Of the 6,000 fishable lakes in the state, none is more appealing to the walleye angler than Lake Mille Lacs. This 132,000-acre lake is the second largest in the state, producing one of every eight pounds of walleye caught each year in Minnesota.

While the walleyes deposit 20 billion eggs into Mille Lacs every year through natural spawning, the angler invests more than 3 million hours on the lake in search of the trophy fish. To extend their odds, up to 6,000 fish houses are transported each winter across the ice through hundreds of miles of plowed lake roads. The result is an annual catch that nears 500,000 pounds of walleye.

It all started as a hobby show hosted by the Lutheran Senior Citizens Home in Little Falls in the late 1960s. While crafting kept the hands and minds of the elders busy, their work was displayed and sold at a nearby school gymnasium. As the annual event grew in popularity, local artists would secure permission to share their crafts at the senior's show. Local merchants began sponsoring the event which was then moved outdoors and downtown. By 1972, the event became so big it was turned over to the Little Falls Area Chamber of Commerce.

The present population of Little Falls is 7,700. But one weekend each September, the Arts & Crafts Fair hosts more than 900 vendors who showcase their crafts to more than 100,000 frantic shoppers who flood the streets, several dressed in matching t-shirts to avoid separation, and celebrate the experience. The festival is one of the largest of its kind in the Upper Midwest. This show is consistently listed as one of the top 200 shows in the nation by *Sunshine Artist Magazine* and continues to be selected as one of the Minnesota Office of Tourism's top 25 group tour festivals in the state of Minnesota.

With less than 500 wild Siberian Tigers remaining on earth, experts fear the species will go extinct by 2010. Of the 180 captive cats in America, one named Kitty lives at the Pine Grove Zoo in Little Falls. Serving as home to a variety of exotic native and domestic animals, this is the only zoo in central Minnesota. It is open year-round, and is free to the public with donations encouraged. Seen here is Bennett Rustad with his new hedgehog friend Nascar.

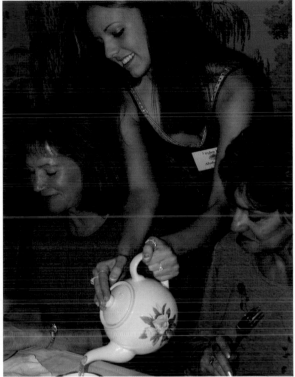

Two large four-story mansions in Little Falls overlook the bluffs of the Mississippi River. They were built in 1898 for two bachelors named Richard Musser and Charles Weyerhaeuser, who co-managed the Pine Tree Lumber Company for their fathers. Today, these mansions are collectively referred to as Linden Hill. With meticulous detail, they have been restored back to the era of the lumber barons, and are listed on the National Register of Historic Places.

Seen here is Susan Haugen, director of the Linden Hill Conference and Retreat Center. As she welcomes our camera into the Music Room of the Musser mansion, her granddaughter Alysha Broda serves guests at one of their famous Quarterly Tea Retreats. These beautiful homes are available for public tour and group events, including overnight stays.

Minnesota's timber was used to help build America. By the turn of the 20th century, the logging industry in the state peaked with production of more than 2.3 billion board feet of lumber, enough to build 600,000 two-story homes every year. Before the railroad, the Mississippi River was used to float the logs south to the sawmills. "River Pigs" were men that rode the logs and did their best to prevent jamming.

The world's greatest log jam occurred in 1894 just to the north of Little Falls. An estimated four billion board feet of lumber created a seven-mile long jam that measured sixty feet deep and up to 2,500 feet in width. It took more than 150 men, five teams of horses and a steam engine more than six months to break it up.

An old fishing lure called a "Surf Oreno" crafted back in 1912 rested in the hands of Al Baert of Sartell, MN in the summer of 1990. A buyer offered Al three dollars for the piece which was valued at more than one hundred fifty dollars. Al realized at the time that the true value of the lure rested not in its perceived market value, but in the memories assigned to the piece by its owner.

Along with his partner Morry Sauve, the two set out to build a museum filled with donated fishing items to help preserve the Minnesota fishing experience. Today more than 7,000 items are on display at the Minnesota Fishing Museum in Little Falls. Seen here is a collection of wooden lures donated by Kent Frank. Each of these 300 pieces were hand carved and painted by various Minnesota anglers.

In 1899, Evangeline Lodge Land received a B.S. degree in Chemistry from the University of Michigan, and applied for a position teaching science at the high school in Little Falls, Minnesota. From Michigan she traveled by ship, then by train to arrive at her destination, the Antlers Hotel in the heart of Little Falls. Upon arrival at the hotel, she met a local lawyer named Charles Lindbergh, who served as counsel to the Weyerhaeuser Lumber Company and later as U.S. Congressman. After a brief courtship, the two married in 1901 at the home of Evangeline's parents in Detroit. Ten months later, Evangeline returned to Detroit where her uncle, Dr. Edwin Lodge Land, oversaw the birth of the Lindbergh's only child. Charles Augustus, Jr. was born on February 4, 1902.

Evangeline returned to her husband in Little Falls five weeks later where they would raise their son Charles, Jr. in their home along the western banks of the Mississippi River. At the age of three he watched his home burn to the ground. The house was rebuilt on the same foundation and Charles, Jr. spent much of his time as a youth in the house which is now listed on the National Register of Historic Places and open to the public.

At age 18, Charles enrolled at the University of Wisconsin at Madison where he studied engineering. He would not return to Little Falls again until after the Spirit of St. Louis flew him into the history books in 1927. Charles Lindbergh, Jr. was selected by *TIME Magazine* as one of the top 100 most influential people of the 20th century.

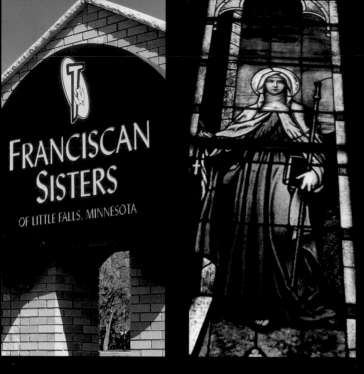

FRANCISCAN SISTERS
OF LITTLE FALLS, MINNESOTA

The Franciscan Sisters of Little Falls, Minnesota are a community of women committed to the Gospel and service to the poor in the spirit of Saints Francis and Clare of Assisi. Founded in 1891, the Sisters started the first hospital in Little Falls, and went on to build and manage many healthcare facilities in Minnesota and other states.

Today the Sisters serve in health care, education, social services, and in pastoral and spiritual ministries that extend to Latin America and Africa. Every year they reunite back at St. Francis Convent in Little Falls to renew ties and deepen their sense of their Franciscan community.

Seen here is Sister Ann Furnstahl who oversees the manufacture and distribution of over three million communion wafers to more than 150 churches in the Upper Midwest.

Months after Minnesota became a territory in 1849, the U.S. government sent a military garrison from Fort Snelling to the newly built Ft. Ripley. Their purpose was to serve as a buffer between feuding bands of Dakota and Ojibwe who had been at war for over 100 years. They were also responsible to oversee the Winnebago Indians relocation from Iowa. The fort, named after War of 1812 hero, Brigadier General Eleazor Ripley, was closed soon after the end of the Civil War. In 1931 the Minnesota National Guard outgrew its 200-acre site at Lake Pepin. With the aid of many of the state's best masons and craftsmen, out of work due to the Depression, Camp Ripley was built. By the early 1960s it had grown from its original 2,000 acres to almost 53,000 acres; nearly six times the size of Gull Lake. This state-of-the-art facility is recognized as one of the finest United States Military installations, providing over 560,000 total training man days to both military and civilian units each year.

Camp Ripley has become an international training site hosting soldiers from as far away as Canada, the United Kingdom, and Norway. Camp Ripley conducts the longest running National Guard troop exchange in existence. For over 30 years more than 100 Norwegian Home Guard soldiers visit the camp for two weeks during February to train in a U.S. Military training center. In turn, about 100 Minnesota National Guard soldiers fly to Norway to experience both the military and cultural differences between the two countries. At arrival, the Norwegians partake in a short briefing regarding plans for the busy two week session. Most training activities are conducted on skis, including day and night ski marches and the annual biathlon.

Camp Ripley's Miller Complex has a first-rate large weapons training area. A sixty-seven ton M1-A1 Abrams Main Battle Tank, similar to the ones used in both of the Gulf Wars, provides a truly dramatic example of fire power as it fires a 120 millimeter shell at a moving target during a combat qualification exercise. Tanks, Bradley Fighting Vehicles, Howitzers, and Multiple Launch Rocket Systems fire live ammunition as the troops prepare for potential battle. Many vacationers around the lakes area hear the low rumble from the distant horizon and ask themselves, "Is that thunder or Ripley?"

Camp Ripley is Minnesota's second largest wildlife refuge. There are numerous programs designed to study the local plant and animal life. One such program is the Black Bear Project, which began in 1989 in response to an increase in nuisance bear complaints from soldiers. Through the use of radio-telemetry and Global Positioning Systems (GPS), bears at Camp Ripley are now monitored for reproductive success, daily and seasonal movements, causes of mortality and interactions with troops in training. Camp Ripley serves as a refuge for possibly 25-30 black bears. The female bear pictured above is

part of an ongoing research project that is coordinated with the Department of Natural Resources Bear Research Group, the University of Minnesota and Medtronic. Bears are monitored during hibernation in order to apply their physiological miracles to human health problems, such as heart disorders. This bear has been tracked since 1999. In that time period, she has had three 3-cub litters, consisting of four males and five females. Pictured, a sleepy cub.

Thousands of soldiers train year-round to become better prepared to serve and protect the United States. Camp Ripley can house up to 10,500 civilian and military trainees at once. Many of the soldiers pictured here are preparing for duty in Kosovo and Bosnia. The extensive training facilities include rappel towers, a biathlon course, firing ranges, and urban assault courses. Because history has shown that lack of preparedness in a hostile winter environment can be disastrous, the National Guard Bureau in Washington D.C. designated Camp Ripley as the primary winter training site for all National Guard units.

Camp Ripley plays host to the Minnesota Military Museum which is open year-round for those interested in learning more about Minnesota's role in the military. In addition, Camp Ripley hosts periodic community events, such as their biannual "Community Appreciation Day." While the young come to pretend, the old often visit to reminisce. At left, the wide-eyed young boy dresses up in a real army uniform. Above, three Pearl Harbor survivors take a moment of silence to remember that infamous day in 1941.

Breeding Wolf Range, 1998

Do the Camp's military activities affect the indigenous gray wolf population? What are the wolf's migration patterns? These are the questions that spurred Camp Ripley's Environmental Supervisor to initiate a study in 1996 to study wolf movements using first-of-their-kind GPS and satellite radio-collars. Since 1996, twenty-five wolves have been radio-collared at Camp Ripley. Currently listed as a federal threatened species and a species of special concern in Minnesota, the gray wolf was found to be more adaptable to human activities than previously thought, crossing freeways and farm fields during their extended travels. The above map highlights a two-year-old female gray wolf that wandered from Camp Ripley all the way through Wisconsin and back again. The wolf traveled over 2,500 miles during the nine-month journey. Research conducted at Camp Ripley also indicates the wolves have become accustomed to military training, adapting their movements and use of habitat according to various troop activities.

An Ohio Army National Guard armor unit assembles on the tarmac at Camp Ripley's airstrip after arriving on a Lockheed C-141C Starlifter. Thousands of other troops have trained at Camp Ripley in preparation for deployment on missions worldwide.

Minnesota State Veterans Cemetery near Camp Ripley

Ten miles to the south of Baxter along State Highway 371 stands a landmark spiral staircase show piece outside the doors of Ironfire Ironworks. For more than twenty years, owners Stan and Cheryl Dobosenski have built this business with the motto, "If it's steel, we can handle it." Pictured here is their apprentice son, Stan, Jr., welding a staircase for yet another customer. Ironfire's creative steel structures include a cable bridge at Tettegouche State Park on the North Shore of Lake Superior, custom railings, fencing, stair systems, structural steel and various other artistic steel objects which are scattered throughout Minnesota and beyond.

Tucked along the east side of State Highway 371, just south of Baxter, sits this well-recognized landmark. Owner Fred Jillson had hoped to move this 1946 Northern Pacific coach car to his property, refurbish it, and convert into an office to be parked adjacent to his home. The day the railcar was delivered, planning and zoning officials followed it into Fred's driveway.

They informed him that zoning laws would prohibit the railcar being parked so close to the road. Fred was forced to move it to the back of his property and scrapped his plans to convert it into his office. Today he seeks a railroad enthusiast willing to acquire this piece of railroad history.

During peak season, an estimated 11,000 vehicles a day will drive by the new Welcome Center heading north into Brainerd/Baxter along State Highway 371. The controversy over handling highway expansion to ease Brainerd bound traffic flow and make for a safer commute is ongoing. One key to the success of the expansion is the safe and environmentally friendly way to clear land.

Meet Puff, a converted corn burner, designed to hurl seventy-five foot balls of flame into unwanted brush piles.

In 1965, Mary Strand watched as her dad Al built a drive-up hamburger stand over her garden bed on the lot next to their home in Pierz, MN. Along with her thirteen younger siblings, Mary began working summer jobs helping her parents serve up cheeseburgers and soft-serve ice cream to the north bound traffic along Highway 25. With Thielen supplying the meat, and Mary's mother Theresa offering up her secret batch of homemade onion rings, Al's Drive-In became an instant hit for the hungry traveler.

Today, the name has changed from Al's to Sue's Drive-In, but the tradition holds for its loyal base of customers. The food remains just as good and the work ethic Al bestowed upon his fourteen kids proved historic. On January 14, 1999, with husband Ralph Kiffmeyer at her side, Al's oldest daughter Mary was sworn in as Minnesota's 20th Secretary of State.

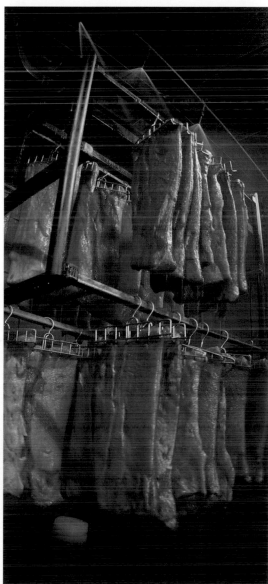

In 1922, a resident of Pierz, MN, Phil Thielen, decided to open a small meat market in the back of a downtown furniture store. He began flavoring meats with a signature hardwood smoking process that has remained a Thielen family secret for more than eighty years. Today, his three great grandsons, Joe, Andy and Matt, along with their dad, Keith, have transformed the business into one of the largest bacon-by-mail suppliers in the United States. Each week they mail out more than 9,000 pounds of bacon nationwide.

neighboring

GULL LAKE

Since 1991 it has been the world's largest party on ice! Up to 12,000 anglers from around the world compete for over $150,000 in cash and prizes at Hole-in-the-Day Bay on Gull Lake in the Brainerd Jaycees Ice Fishing Extravaganza. Confidence Learning Center, a year-round center for people with developmental disabilities, receives a portion of the proceeds.

(Far left) On August 2, 2003 Camp Confidence sponsored the 1st annual Brainerd Lake's Fishing Has No Boundaries event where anglers with disabilities spent the day with a fishing guide trying to catch the big one. Andy Herold was one of the lucky anglers who caught this beautiful Northern Pike while fishing with Dan "The Walleye Man" Eigen.

Breathtaking beauty defines this panoramic view of the eighth hole on The Classic at Madden's Golf Course. The combination of wildlife, water and woods embodies the championship style of golf course designed along the Brainerd Golf Trail by some of the greatest names in golf, including Arnold Palmer and Robert Trent Jones. With more than 450 holes of golf within close proximity, today's Brainerd Lakes region has become the Midwest's #1 golf and resort destination.

In the early 1930s, Jack and Jim Madden pioneered the golf boom by owning and promoting the first 18-hole course in the Brainerd Lakes area. In turn, they worked to encourage other local resort owners to follow their lead by attracting golfers as well as anglers to the north woods. In 1991, Grand View Lodge opened The Pines, which became the first area course professionally designed for championship golf. Today there are five Brainerd area courses that have been nationally recognized by *Golf Digest, Golf Week, Golf and Travel,* and *Golf Magazine.*

Once a stronghold for the fishing industry, the Brainerd
Lakes area has now expanded to include the golfing
community. The impact of these two industry giants that
now share the lake country was no more evident than
when the City of Pequot Lakes discussed repainting their
legendary bobber water tower to look like a golf ball.
Although the change was never implemented, it was a
sign that golfers were now on par with the anglers as
equal draws for the tourism dollar.

The last remnants of ice melt away on the Brainerd area lakes around mid-April, signaling an annual rite of spring for cabin owners — putting in the dock and boat lifts. Beau and Dane from D.H. Docks & Tracks brave the cool and misty early spring weather during a new dock and lift installation on Gull Lake's Hunters Point.

The Gull Lake Dam was built in 1911-1912
bringing an end to the logging era in the Gull
Lake Chain. The dam is a barrier for
thousands of walleyes that annually migrate
upriver in the spring from the Crow Wing
and Gull Rivers in search of a place to
spawn. After the walleyes spawn, many
remain at the Gull Lake Dam site until
mid-summer. This concentration of walleyes
draws hundreds of dedicated anglers to the
banks of the Gull River in an annual ritual
that occurs on the second weekend in May.
To protect the concentrated spawning
walleye populations, fishing immediately
below the dam is off limits. That doesn't stop
eager anglers who come early Friday
evening, hours before the Minnesota Fishing
Opener officially commences at 12:01 a.m.,
to stake their claim for the best spot
available to catch the elusive walleye.

SPAWNING
AREA
NO FISHING
NO BOATING

Marv Koep guides Kellan Johnson on Clark Lake.

Marv Koep, an area fishing icon and guide for over 40 years, moved to Nisswa with wife Judy in 1961 to start the legendary Koep's Nisswa Bait and Tackle, more commonly referred to as Koep's. At first they only sold minnows, but later added tackle, Lowrance depth finders, and guide services. Marv founded the Nisswa Guides League in 1967, giving many guides their start, including Al and Ron Lindner, Harry VanDorn, Max Slocum, Cully Swenson, Bob Collette, Royal Karels, and Rod Romine. On a September morning, soon after the Nisswa Guides League was created, five of the guides (Marv Koep, Max Slocum,

Al Lindner, Ron Lindner, and Cully Swenson) had a friendly fishing contest on Gull Lake which resulted in this haul of seventeen walleye limits. Soon after this photo was first published, sales of Lindy Tackle sky-rocketed, and Marv Koep's career took off. His life-long accomplishments were aptly recognized when Marv was inducted into the Freshwater Fishing Hall of Fame as a "Legendary Guide" in 1999 and into the Minnesota Fishing Hall of Fame in 2000.

Fourth of July fireworks at Grand View Lodge

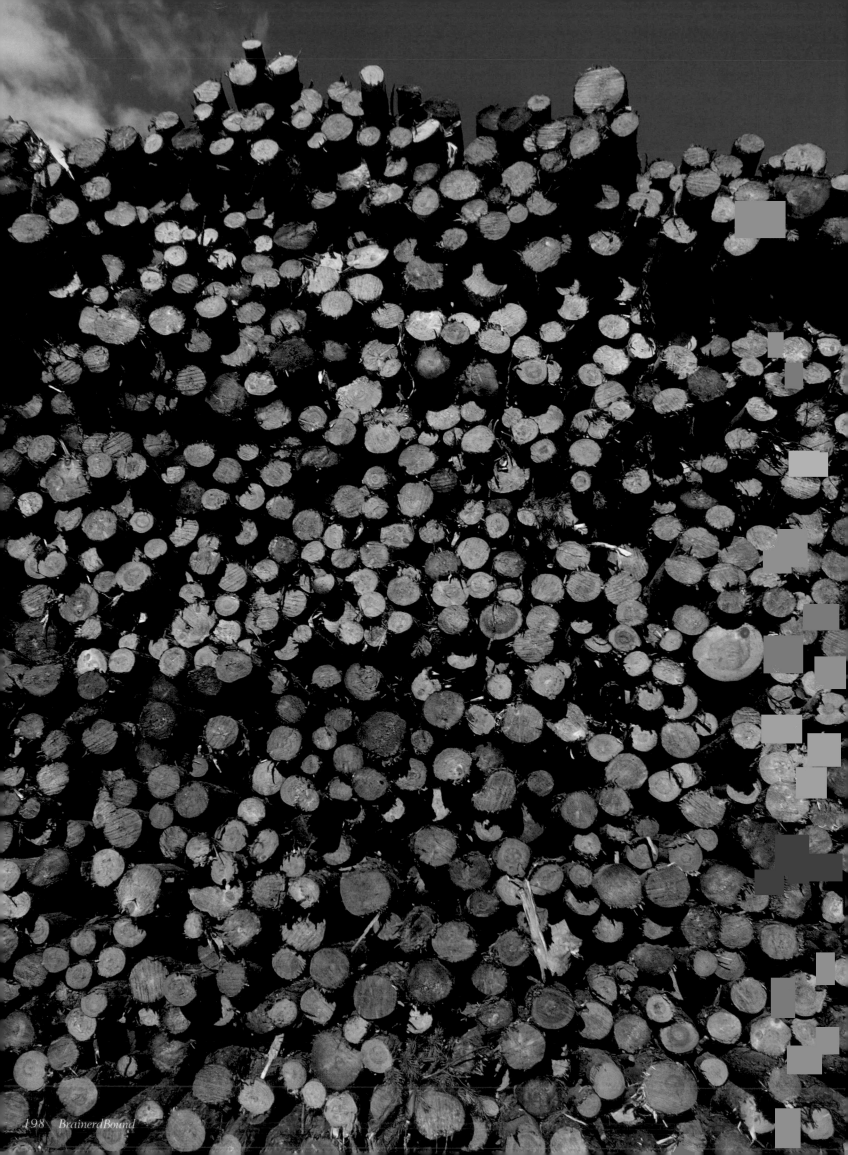

After a long day of cutting timber, lumberjacks Desirae, Dominique and Dallin Sonenstahl of Pine River pose for the camera before taking a ride down Main Street at Nisswa's Winter Jubilee celebration.

With his dream cabin half built, A.J. Lutter sat behind the wheel of a county truck sealing cracks in the highway. To fight the boredom, he began whittling wood, which lead him to the local craft shows to test the market. He soon realized that the "carve or starve" approach would mean going bigger and faster with his art. A short stint as a lumberjack soon put a chainsaw into his hands, where he carved an old indian head on lunch break that he sold for $35. A.J. began to build an inventory of chainsaw art, but wouldn't see sales jump until he began doing carvings live in front of his audience.

Today his work can be seen at various craft shows and state fairs throughout the Upper Midwest, and displayed at his famous "Come See What I Saw" storefront along State Highway 371. When asked how he is able to carve such wonderful work, A.J. replies: "The work is already in the wood. I just cut away what doesn't belong."

A Brainerd area vacationer waits her turn to slide down the waterslide at the Nisswa Family Fun Center. In 2004 owner Don McFarland added five rides from the now closed Paul Bunyan Amusement Center.

Max Rustad makes the putt on the eighth hole of the Captain's Course at Pirate's Cove Adventure Golf. It is one of twenty-five Pirate's Cove courses in the United States and one of the few adventure golf courses in Minnesota.

During peak season, almost 200 vendors showcase their crafts and antiques to more than 5,000 weekend bargain hunters at the Nisswa Flea Market.

One such vendor has spent the past ten years showcasing his handcrafted furniture to the crowds. Meet Merle Mathison (bottom), an octogenarian from Lake Shore, as he proudly displays the products he creates without the benefit of sight. Merle suffers from glaucoma and is legally blind.

The remnants of the logging industry pushing railroads deeper into the north woods a century ago left in their wake a railroad bed that stretches 210 miles from Brainerd to the Canadian border. Today's Paul Bunyan Trail is built atop the first 110 miles of that track, linking Baxter to Bemidji for snowmobilers, bikers, inline skaters and hikers. The paved trail weaves its way through twenty-one lakes, across nine rivers and streams, and through some of Minnesota's most scenic countryside. Plans are in the works to extend the paved trail to Crow Wing State Park, the Cuyuna Lakes Trail, and the Blue Ox Trail extending from Bemidji to International Falls.

the Paul Bunyan Trail.

BRAINERD-BEMIDJI
Minnesota

With an eight-foot wing span, the Trumpeter Swan is the largest waterfowl in North America, where more than 16,000 make their home. They build nests up to twelve feet in diameter, mate for life and return each year to their same nest. Seen here is Gracie. She and her mate Rex make their home at the Paul Bunyan Learning Center. Since 1993, this 104-acre educational center has played host to school groups, 4H clubs, scouts and family vacationers year round. Their motto, "Come Learn With Us" delivers nature programs that help protect the future of the Brainerd area wildlife.

Minnesota's largest motor sports celebration is held each August at the National Hot Rod Association event at Brainerd International Raceway. The week's events draw more than 100,000 spectators who come to see the biggest names in drag racing. This series is unique because it's the only form of sports where fans can gain access to the "locker room," get autographs from the drivers and watch as crews prepare their machines for competition in the pits.

Seen here is six-time NHRA champion Kenny Bernstein ready to begin the burnout procedure in his 6,500 hp nitromethane-powered Budweiser/Lucas Oil Top Fuel dragster. Kenny will accelerate down the world-class quarter-mile race track reaching top speeds of more than 330 mph.

Between qualifying runs and on race day, Kenny returns to the pits after each race where his crew will disassemble and reassemble the engine and clutch within the allotted seventy-five minutes. The sensory overload from the smell of the nitromethane, the deafening sound of the engines, and the feel of the ground-pounding cars vibrating through the spectators' bones draws them back year after year.

Today, Brainerd International Raceway (BIR) is more than a world-class drag strip. The 800-acre site also houses a three-mile road course and a campground that features 160 full-service RV sites. Racing extends to Gokarts, Superbikes, Lawnmowers, and MotoCross, and in 2004, BIR will host a first ever NASCAR feeder race for the Winston Cup. Each Wednesday night through the summer, BIR also hosts street drags. Any owner of a street-legal car can come race on the track.

While BIR's facility is seen as world-class within the national racing community, it's increasingly becoming more family focused, drawing fans from throughout the Midwest. BIR works hard to break down the barriers that separate its events from the local community and strives to expand its fan base into the lake country by offering a fun family weekend to local residents and vacationers.

Founded in 1958, North Central Speedway is
sometimes overlooked by the Brainerd Lakes'
vacationers, but not by the approximately 2,000 locals
who show up on Saturdays for a chance to get close
to the drivers and the non-stop racing action. Over
twenty race events are held from May to September
on this one-third mile semi-banked clay oval track.

Located in the heart of the Brainerd Lakes area, not too far from the numerous upscale specialty retailers, the Second Time Around store stands out as a place to buy, sell, or trade about anything you can imagine. For over 19 years, Mary Sample-Andersen has made a successful business out of selling other people's unwanted home furnishings. The eclectic items offered in this second-hand store make it a favorite of locals and tourists alike in the Brainerd area. Once you set foot into the store, you're hooked and just might become one of Mary's many regulars.

Not all the old-fashioned bait shops have disappeared from the Brainerd Lakes area. When you walk into S&W Bait and Tackle and see the tanks brimming with a variety of minnows, the walls covered with snapshots of the "big one," and coffee brewing for their customers, you know you are in the right place. Cliff Wicktor and Sherree Stillings Wicktor moved to Brainerd in 1988 to open the bait shop. Marv Koep, one of the areas well-known fishing guides and bait shop owners, stopped by frequently to offer support and advice. Although Sherree's husband Cliff and son C.J. are no longer with them, she and her son Frankie plan on running the store the way they always have, with old-fashioned friendly service.

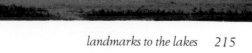

A well-known native of Minnesota, Babe Winkelman started fishing on the farm he grew up on at the age of six and has been fishing nonstop ever since. His enthusiasm for fishing and hunting grew into his dream career. As the host of two national, award-winning television shows, "Outdoor Secrets" and "Good Fishing," Babe continues to teach others the art of fishing and hunting and the importance of conservation. Honors include his induction into the Sports Legends Hall of Fame in 1992, the Minnesota Fishing Hall of Fame in 2001, and the Fresh Water Fishing Hall of Fame in 1998. Babe continues to educate and encourage others to hunt and fish through his television shows, newspaper articles, videos, DVDs, books and personal appearances.

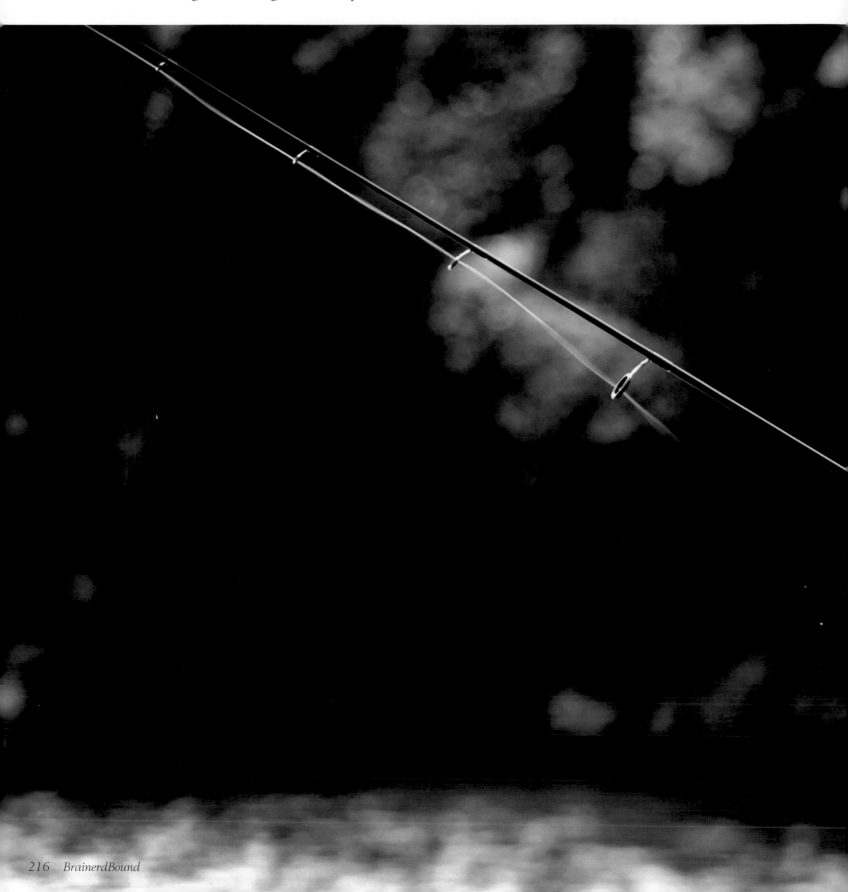

Father and son ice fish on Gull Lake.

Contributing Photographers:
Master Sgt. Charles Farrow,
  Pages 162, 163, 169
Doug Hetland, Pages 108, 112
Bill Horn, Page 122
Steve Pohls, Pages 106, 208-209
Bill Lindner Photography,
  Pages 14-15, 141, 185
Bill Marchel, Page 206
Nels Norquist, Pages 33, 216-217
Peter Wong, Pages 186-187
101st Airborne Division, Page 167

Vintage Images Supplied by:
Breezy Point Resort, Page 24
Cradle of Aviation Museum,
  Garden City, NY, Page 155
Cragun's Resort and Hotel, Page 25
Croft Mine Historical Park,
  Pages 100, 102-103, 105, 107
Crow Wing Historical Society,
  Pages 24, 38-39
Gretchen Finnerty, Page 97
Grand View Lodge, Page 24
Brock Holbert, Page 97
Hochmayr Family, Page 96
Kavanaugh's Resort and Restaurant,
  Page 25
Mary Kiffmeyer, Page 180
Lakes Area Gallery, Pages 46-47
Lindy Legendary Fishing Tackle,
  Page 95
Madden's on Gull Lake, Page 25
Don and Patti McFarland, Pages 25, 96
Mills Fleet Farm, Page 24
Morrison County Historical Society,
  Pages 97, 150-151
Bob and Judy Perrizo, Page 97
Ruttger's Bay Lake Lodge, Page 24
Van Essen Family, Page 97

Contributing Organizations:
Applied Graphics
Babe Winkelman Productions
Bang Printing
Becker Furniture World
Bill Lindner Photography
Brainerd Action Group
Brainerd Lakes Area Chamber of
  Commerce
Brainerd City Directory
Brainerd Daily Dispatch
Brainerd Helicopter Service
Brainerd International Raceway
Brainerd Jaycees
Breezy Point Ice Arena
Breezy Point Resort

Burlington Northern Sante Fe
Camp Confidence
Camp Knutson
Camp Ripley
Central Lakes College Photography Class
Charles A. Lindbergh Foundation
Charles A. Lindbergh House Historic Site
Charles A. Lindbergh State Park
Charles A. Weyerhaeuser Memorial
  Museum
Clearwater Travel Plaza
Cragun's Resort and Hotel on Gull Lake
Creative Wood Products
Croft Mine Historical Park
Crosby Ironton Courier
Crosslake Chamber of Commerce
Crow Wing Historical Society
Crow Wing State Park
Cuyuna Country Heritage Preservation
  Society
Cuyuna Range Chamber of Commerce
Cuyuna Regional Medical Center
D.H. Docks & Tracks
Dallman Signs
exploreminnesota.com
Gander Mountain
Garrison Sports
Garrison Sports Club
Gemini Research
Goff & Howard
Gold'n Plump
Grand Casino Mille Lacs
Grand View Lodge
Houston Aeros (AHL)
Ideal Fire Department
KAJ Graphics
Kathio State Park
Kavanaugh's Resort and Restaurant
Kenny Bernstein Budweiser King Racing
Linden Hill Conference Center
Lindner's Angling Edge
Little Falls Chamber of Commerce
Little Falls Convention & Visitors Bureau
Little Rock Boat Works
Madden's on Gull Lake
Maple Leaf Photography
McDonald's Meats
Midwest Captions
Mille Lacs Band of Ojibwe
Mille Lacs Tourism Council
Mills Fleet Farm
Minnesota Army National Guard
Minnesota Correctional Facility-St. Cloud
Minnesota Department of Corrections
Minnesota Department of Economic
  Development
Minnesota Department of Natural

Resources
Minnesota Department of Transportation
Minnesota Fishing Hall of Fame
Minnesota Fishing Museum
Minnesota Historical Society
Minnesota Lakes Association
Minnesota Military Museum
Minnesota Office of Tourism
Minnesota Raptor Center
Minnesota School of Diving
Minnesota Wild
Morrison County Historical Society
Nelson Nursery
Nelson-Mitchell Advertising Outfitters
New Mexico Museum of Space History
NHL/AHL
NHRA
Nisswa Chamber of Commerce
Nisswa Flea Market
North Central Speedway
Northbound Antiques
Norwegian Home Guard
Oakwood Game Farm
Ohio National Guard
Oliver Kelly Farm
Our Place
Paul Bunyan Amusement Center
Paul Bunyan Land at This Old Farm
  Pioneer Village
Paul Bunyan Nature Learning Center
Paul Bunyan Scenic Byway Association
Pequot Lakes Chamber of Commerce
Performance Promotions
Peterson Potato Farm
Pine Grove Zoo
Pirates Cove Adventure Golf
Point of Perfection Figure Skating Camp
Range Printing
Ruttger's Bay Lake Lodge
S&W Bait and Tackle
Second Time Around
Sherburne County Historical Society
Sherburne National Wildlife Refuge
St. Cloud Park and Recreation
St. Cloud Convention & Visitors Bureau
The Franciscan Sisters of Little Falls
The Pines at Grand View Lodge
Treasure City
Twin City Powerboat Association
U.S. Department of Interior
University of Minnesota Raptor Center
University of Minnesota Tourism Center
Woodtick Inn
World Snowmobile Association
Xcel Energy

Special thanks to:
Patt Adair
Carol Altepeter
Jeff Arnold
Al Baert
Jessie Betting
Dave Black
Tom and Emilie Boelz
Mary (Cote) Boos
Tim Brastrup
Todd Bymark
Vojta Cervenka
Dutch and Irma Cragun
Julie DeJong
Stan Dobosenski and Family
LeeAnn Doucette
Dan Eigen
Julie Engelmeyer
Joey Erickson
Master Sgt. Charles Farrow
Joe Fellegy
Jim Friedrich
Bruce Fuhrman
Sister Ann Furnstahl
Doreen Gallaway
Linda Gettelman
Geoff Gorvin
Lance Hamilton
Bob and Ruth Ann Hanson
Bruce Hanson
Susan Haugen
Mike Hehner
Doug Hetland
Hochmayr Family
Brock Holbert
Jeanne Holler
Bill Horn
Stephanie Huseby
Dan Jacobson
Lloyd Jacobson
Robert Janski
Peggy Jensen
Fred Jillson
Karen Johnson
Rodger Johnston
Jeff Jones
Master Sgt. Leonard Kallsen
Frank Kasowski
John Kavanaugh
Paul Keiski
Mary Kiffmeyer
Michael Knapp
Albert Knieff
Marv Koep
Steve Kohls
Jeff Kreitz

Al Lindner and Family
Ron Lindner and Family
Al Lohman
Glen Lommel
Dr. Duane R. Lund
Matt Majka
Cathy Malecha
Richard Mark
Bill Matthies
McDonald Family
Don and Patti McFarland
Doug McFarland
Terry McGaughey
Jim Meyer and Family
Iona Miller
Stewart C. Mills, Jr.
David Milne
Elsie Mooer
Kathy Moore
Richard Mooth
Nels Norquist
Craig Oleen
Chris and Mary Ann Olson
Julie O'Shaughnessy
Lisa Paxton
Bob and Judy Perrizo
Pam Perry
Radermacher family
Mike Ramsey
Carol Reamer
Cecilia Riedl
Sister Elizabeth Roberts
Mark Ronnei
Barb Rustad
Elizabeth Rustad
Jack Ruttger
Louise Salo
Mary Sample-Andersen
Lynn Scharenbroich
Ron Schultz
Major Joseph Seaquist
Bob Slaybaugh
Kathryn Smith
Pete Smith
Donna Sonenstahl and Family
Jim Spielman
Bob Spizzo
Bailey Stone
Keith Thielen and family
Staff Sgt. Rebecca Thingvold
Becky Thorpe
Deb (Madden) Thuringer
Bonnie Tweed
Cintra Utter
Dorothy Utter
Eric Utter

Mark Van Essen
Mary Warner
David Watts
Lt. Col. Richard Weaver
Steve Weber
Mark Welch
Bob White
Nate Whited
Sherree Wicktor
Babe Winkelman
Wayne Zitzow
Hub Zyvoloski

Publications Referenced:
A Family of Pioneers, by Albert Knieff
Brainerd Daily Dispatch
Cuyuna! A Chronical of the Cuyuna Range,
  by Cuyuna Range Bicentennial
  Committee
Gull Lake: Yesterday and Today, by
  Dr. Duane R. Lund
History of Stearns County; Volume 1, by
  William Bell Mitchell
Mike and Ike and Morningtown, by
  David Umhauer and Kurt Haubrich
Old Crow Wing: History of a Village, by
  Bernard Coleman
Oldtimers I, by Carl Zapffe
Oldtimers II, by Carl Zapffe
Tales of Four Lakes, by Duane R. Lund
*The First 100 Years: Ruttger's Bay Lake
  Lodge*, by Mae Ruttger Heglund

Sunset closes another season at
Velvet Beach

The sun sets along Wildlife Drive at the Sherburne
National Wildlife Reserve